BILL EASUM
PETE THEODORE

THE
NOMADIC
CHURCH

GROWING YOUR CONGREGATION
WITHOUT OWNING THE BUILDING

ABINGDON PRESS / Nashville

THE NOMADIC CHURCH
GROWING YOUR CONGREGATION WITHOUT OWNING THE
BUILDING

Library of Congress Cataloging-in-Publication Data

Easum, William M., 1939-
  The nomadic church : growing your congregation without owning the building / Bill Easum and Pete Theodore.
    p. cm.
  ISBN 0-687-49700-0 (pbk. : alk. paper)
  1. Church facilities. I. Theodore, Pete, 1972- II. Title.

  BV604.E37 2005
  254'.7—dc22   2005002129

05 06 07 08 09 10 11 12 13 14—10 9 8 7 6 5 4 3 2 1

MANUFACTURED IN THE UNITED STATES OF AMERICA

With love to our precious wives, Karen Theodore and Jan Easum (Proverbs 12:4a; 31:10);

to the courageous churches who "go and make disciples" in rented facilities (Matthew 28:18-20);

and to the many Nomadic Churches who allowed us to draw upon their hard-earned wisdom for this book (Proverbs 11:14; 15:22).

All of you are tangible manifestations of God's supreme grace, goodness, and glory!

What is this place where we are meeting?
Only a house, the earth its floor,
walls and roof sheltering people,
windows for light, an open door.
Yet it becomes a body that lives
when we are gathered here,
and know our Lord is near. . . .

This is the place where we can receive
what we need to increase:
God's justice and God's peace.

This excerpt from an untitled early Anabaptist hymn was originally published in Valerius's Neder-Landische Gedenckklanck *(Zürich: n.p., 1626).*

CONTENTS

FOREWORD

Visionaries are a major pain in the neck. They get a big idea and get people all hyped up to do something about it. People with any common sense will run the other way when they see a visionary coming. Especially if the visionary is a church planter!

Unless, of course, these people have faith along with their common sense, and they believe the vision is good and will further God's will being done on earth. Then, people with common sense and uncommon faith will respond to the vision, plunge in, and get involved.

But even so, visionaries are a pain in the neck because, although they have this great vision, they generally have no idea of how many details must be dealt with, how many laws must be complied with, how many risks must be anticipated, how many problems must be solved, how many dollars must be not only raised but also accounted for, and how many hours must be invested behind the scenes for their vision to become reality.

I know what a pain visionaries are because I am one. People have been telling me for years that I make their lives a lot more difficult (maybe a little more exciting and fruitful too?) every time I say, "Hey, I have an idea!" I have been fortunate—no, downright *blessed* is the only right word for it—to be surrounded by people who deal with the thousand necessities that my visionary adventures entail. My brother, Pete, is one of them.

We planted a church back in the 1980s—we meaning my wife and I and nine other people. It started in a home, then moved to

1

a middle school, then to an elementary school, then to a high school, then to a college, then back to a high school, then temporarily to a couple of elementary and middle schools—and *finally* to our own property. For seventeen years we were a Nomadic Church. That means that we met approximately 884 times in rented facilities on Sundays alone (well, a few less, because the janitor would occasionally forget to show up and we'd have to do church on the sidewalk). Add midweek and special meetings, and the number tops a thousand, I'm sure.

My brother Pete wasn't one of the original eleven, but very early on, he and his intrepid wife, Karen, and their three children became part of the adventure. Pete became one of the heroes of the "set-up team," which was also the "take-down team," which was also the "sound team," which was also the "lighting team," and so on. When I think what they have given and sacrificed through the years—when I think of the weight my brother has lifted!—I am humbled, amazed, and grateful to God.

My guess is that you need about 150 Petes for every one of me. The needed quota of visionary activist preachers seems easy to come by. However, faithful, dedicated, hard-working, noncomplaining, resourceful, flexible, and—did I say faithful?—people like Pete are much harder to find. They get up at 4:00 or 5:00 A.M. Sunday after Sunday to drive a truck to the meeting place, unload it, set up sound equipment, solve electrical glitches, maybe serve as the mixer at the sound board for a few hours (while the preacher drones on and on), and then pack up and reload the truck, drive it back to its parking place, and get home hopefully before dinnertime. They aren't late. They don't complain (much). They sweat. They don't get paid a dime!

Over the years, some of these hard-working people burn out. Some get bitter. Some get injured or simply exhausted, or perhaps their spouses or kids say, "Enough is enough!" A Nomadic Church can't run without them!

What would happen if somebody did some research that focused not on the visionary church leaders with all their big ideas about church planting, but on the Petes of the world who make those ideas come to life—who literally put wheels on those big ideas? What if someone tried to compile those people's accumulated wisdom about doing church in schools, hotels, recreation centers, restaurants, or other nontraditional places? You would come up with a book like the one you're holding now.

The potential benefits of this book could be truly staggering. People who would have been burned out now won't be. People who would have been overworked will have ways of sharing the load and building teams. People who would have been frustrated will avoid more mistakes, have more fun, and experience more joy. People who wouldn't have thought of some creative ideas on their own will get to put those ideas into practice and they, along with their whole congregation, will reap the benefits. Plus, people like Pete will be better appreciated.

In our journey here at Cedar Ridge Community Church, there have been a lot of heroes like Pete: Bruce, Eric, Ron, Rob, and so many more (including all their spouses!). They didn't have the advantage of a book like this. They had to invent everything as they went along. By the grace of God, they survived our seventeen-year sojourn, and did so with a good spirit. Knowing how much they've suffered and sacrificed, I'm all the more grateful for the work Bill Easum and another Pete—Pete Theodore—have done.

Because of economic and real estate realities in many places in the world, especially many of the places most needing church planting (like inner cities), it may be that Nomadic Churches won't be a temporary (seventeen years didn't feel like temporary!) step toward a permanent home: They may be permanently nomadic! What's more, increasing numbers of church planters are envisioning never owning their own facilities for strategic and missional reasons. For these situations, the practical wisdom distilled in these pages will be priceless.

I didn't mean to insult visionaries in my opening remarks. Obviously, I think they (we) have some value. But as time goes on, we realize more and more that teams make churches fly, and those teams must include people with practical gifts—service, hospitality, organization, planning, administration, and the like. I thank God that resources like this one are being produced by and for these important people.

I think of the story in the Gospels about Palm Sunday. Jesus needed to enter Jerusalem on a donkey to fulfill a prophetic vision from the Old Testament. He sent some disciples into Bethphage and Bethany to borrow a donkey. We all know the story—the crowds, the coats, the palm branches, the shouts, the rocks not crying out.

Now imagine the day is over, the excitement has died down, and the disciples are just falling asleep somewhere. Suddenly, an unnamed disciple (like my brother) wakes up with a start and whacks himself in the forehead. "What's wrong?" a fellow disciple asks. "Who's going to return the donkey?" the crestfallen disciple replies. Then he gets up and loses a night's sleep returning the donkey to its owner, as promised.

Behind every great and holy story, there are donkeys that need to be returned. This is a book about those necessities, a book for the practical, down-to-earth, make-it-happen folk to read and put into practice. It would be very good for visionary church-planter-types to read it too. They'll better appreciate the Petes among them who put wheels on the grand God-given visions they receive and pass on.

One of the things I like most about Pete is that he has a good sense of humor. I can't count how many times—in spite of last-minute equipment failures and other frustrations—he and his team could be heard laughing, making jokes, and turning hard work into good fun. Those nomadic years were hard years, but they were good years.

I remain a firm believer in the importance of church planting. Yes, I am for church revitalizations wherever they can occur, but church planting always has been and will continue to be an essential element of the mission of Jesus Christ. It is my honor to introduce and commend this book that will make church planting more doable and, I hope, more enjoyable (can I say fun?) too.

Brian McLaren
www.anewkindofchristian.com
www.crcc.org
www.emergentvillage.com

Who Will Benefit from Reading *The Nomadic Church*?

Those whom this book will most directly equip and encourage include:

- Pastors and leaders of churches who currently meet in temporary facilities for worship services and other ministries.

- Any church planter who will use rented facilities.

- Anyone feeling called to start a church or be part of a church planting team.

- Those who lead or want to begin multiple-campus churches, cell-based churches, satellite churches, house churches, citywide churches, and other ministries that grow more quickly, efficiently, and economically by using multiple meeting sites.

- Parachurch leaders whose ministries involve the regular use of rented facilities.

- Leaders of established churches that need to meet in temporary quarters between building projects or due to displacement (for example, by natural disaster or fire).

- Christian schools and educational institutes who use temporary facilities.

- Denominational leaders and others who oversee church planting efforts or movements especially in the U.S.

- Church consultants whose clientele includes churches without their own building or campus.

What Assumptions Underlie *The Nomadic Church*?

Everybody brings some presuppositions to their research and writing efforts, whether they admit it or not. We have chosen to make several of our fundamental assumptions clear from the outset.

- Those reading this book have a commitment to Jesus Christ that gives direction to all that they are and do.

- Christian scholarship (thinking) and practice (doing) should not be polarized or dichotomized (e.g., Ezra 7:10; Ps 119:33-34; Matt 5:19; 22:37; Luke 1:1-4; 1 Cor 14:20; 2 Tim 2:2; 1 Pet 3:15). Accordingly, this book subtly seeks to marry both elements toward the ultimate end of glorifying God (e.g., Ps 86:8-13; John 12:28; Rom 5:5-13; 11:36; 1 Cor 6:20; 10:31; 1 Pet 4:11; Rev 4:11).

- The physical housing situation of a particular church is not neutral but has an impact on its ministry in both negative and positive ways.

- How a church responds to its housing context largely determines whether its cumulative effect is negative or positive.

- It is valid, necessary, and productive to study and understand every actual or potential phase in the life cycle of a local church, including any period it may exist without a permanent physical campus.

- A Christian congregation should physically and corporately meet together on a regular basis in some place (e.g., Acts 2:1, 46; 20:7; 1 Cor 11:18, 34; 14:23-34; Heb 10:25). The question in this study is not whether they should do so, but, if they do so in rented facilities, what challenges might they face and how can they intelligently respond to them.

- A local church can and should learn from the biblical record and the successes and failures of other local churches, and this shared knowledge can advance the whole church of Jesus Christ.

- Applying the knowledge gained through exercising the previous presuppositions can stimulate churches to better fulfill their biblical mission while conserving their limited resources.

It is our hope that this book will equip you to recognize and overcome the facility-related challenges you will face as you begin, build, and birth local churches. Enjoy the journey!

Bill Easum
Port Aransas, Texas

Pete Theodore
Portland, Oregon

Impossible Dreams Do Come True!

Seneca Creek Community Church (www.senecacreek.org) in Germantown, Maryland, was just a gleam in Bruce and Jacquie's hearts in 1988. Bruce was still in seminary when God planted the dream of starting a culturally relevant church in a major metropolitan area that would specifically target unchurched people by using contemporary music, penetrating drama, and life-changing, relevant messages.

However, their dream did not stop there. Beyond reaching unchurched people with the gospel of Jesus Christ, they also wanted to build up those new believers in Christ and then train them to do the same with others.

Before finishing seminary and moving to the new location, Bruce and Jacquie organized a team to pray for this new church venture. At the top of their prayer list was a request for a couple to move with them. Specifically, they prayed that the husband would be a great keyboard player with a heart for discipleship and some experience in Christian education. Shortly thereafter, Mark and Diane Tindle transferred into the church where Bruce had been working. Their prayer had been answered; Mark fit the profile perfectly.

Possible things don't need God. Only that which seems impossible needs God.

Upon graduating in June of 1989, Bruce, Jacquie, and their four-month-old daughter, Chelsea, made a parachute drop into the Washington, D.C., area. A little over a month later, Mark and Diane Tindle joined them to begin Seneca Creek Community Church. They had limited funds and even fewer contacts in the area. About all they really had was a dream—and a big God!

Fifteen years and nine locations later, Seneca Creek is among the ten largest churches in the area and still meets in Seneca Valley High School for worship services. They remodeled space in a strip mall to serve as a Ministry Center that accommodates their large staff and a midweek teaching service, and they've very recently purchased a 105-acre tract of land that they've been eyeing for years. They support local upstart churches, mentor area church planters, and regularly send teams and money to help start new churches in Nigeria and Peru.

This Nomadic Church, like so many others we've run across lately, is living evidence that impossible dreams do come true.

CHAPTER ONE

WHY THE NOMADIC CHURCH?

I t's 5:30 A.M. on Sunday. A van backs up cautiously to a darkened high school, followed closely by a well-worn compact car. A handful of adults and a sleepy teen emerge from the two vehicles and begin unloading boxes and equipment from the van. For the next couple of hours this crew joins forces with musicians, teachers, and other servants to turn a high school building into a church building. By 8:00 A.M. they are ready for the first round of people to file through their doors, unaware of all the sacrifices that have already been made to pave their way. At 12:45 P.M. the same vehicles back up to the school, and the same people fill them with the same containers they unloaded only hours before. This faithful band of Levites drives away to store everything and gets ready to do it all again the next Sunday.

This unglamourous ritual is re-enacted thousands of times every weekend across the U.S. Each week platoons of the faithful converge on various "atypical" congregational meeting sites. With the precision of veteran stagehands, they transform rented schools, theaters, community centers, warehouses, gymnasiums, and other unlikely places into functional worship settings. Some are fortunate to have trucks and trailers; others have to cope with only cars. But all of them boil with passion to fulfill the Great Commission. We call these vagabond congregations the "Nomadic Church."

The Nomadic Church

A remarkable thing began happening in the final years of the twentieth century. God began directing more and more pastors to bypass the traditional method of planting churches and instead start "Nomadic Churches"—congregations that meet for years in temporary facilities without the cumbersome burden of huge debts incurred from buying land and property at the outset. They focus on building lives and communities instead of building with bricks and mortar. They are shackled to the majestic Builder, not chained to mere buildings.

The Nomadic Church, sometimes called a portable church, is defined in this book as a local church that meets in someone else's space, which is not a traditional church building, for an extended period of time in order to conduct corporate worship and other ministries.

The Nomadic Church is no longer the fad of a few; it's a growing trend. Thousands of churches are started in the U.S. each year, and the vast majority of them rent meeting space, many for ten years or longer. That is more than twice as long as a decade ago,[1] and a growing number say they never plan on purchasing property.[2] Consider the comment of Todd Wilson, Executive Pastor of New Life Christian Church (www.newlife4me.net) in Chantilly, Virginia: "We will consider getting our own property when the costs for renting begin to approach the cost of owning our own property."

From the contact information provided on Coal Creek Chapel's Web site: "We would give you our address, but we have no idea where we will be when you read this."[3]

According to a comprehensive 1998 survey, almost 14 percent of all congregations in the U.S. rent space in a school or other public facility (see table 1).[4] An even broader study in 2001 found that 10 percent of churches meeting in a church building rent that space from another church.[5] That study also reports that of all faith communities begun since 1945, nearly half of them began in the 1990s.[6] Because of the upsurge in the cost of construction and because of modifications in ministry philosophy, most of these churches remain without their own campus today. Our observations and networks indicate that this buildingless trend is only increasing since these recent surveys were published.

Table 1: Percentage of U.S. Congregations Meeting in Different Types of Places

Type of Building Used for Corporate Service(s)	Percentage of Congregations Meeting in Each Place
Church Building	86.6%
School	5.2%
Storefront	1.0%
Other*	7.3%
*Nonchurch community center, hotel, theater, private home, restaurant, day-care center, or other place not specified on questionnaire.	

Two decades ago, some thought that these Nomadic Churches were smaller and catered to the lower half of the income structure.[7] But no more. Today, they come in every size and reach every strata of American culture. In fact, with good reason many former negative perceptions of Nomadic Churches have begun to be shed in recent years.

New Hope Christian Fellowship (www.enewhope.org) in Honolulu, Hawaii, is one of the premier examples of a congregation choosing to remain in rented facilities. As of 2003, the average weekend attendance exceeds 1,500 people, including seven satellite sites, and the church still rents worship facilities for all its locations. They see their group of Levites, the crews who set up and break down each weekend, as one of the basic training grounds for future leaders of the church. Every Sunday morning from 2:00 to 5:30, a team of over a hundred people gather to set up for services in the rented Farmington High School, which accommodates up to 8,500 people.

In a 1999 interview with their pastor, Wayne Cordeiro, we asked why they were still in rented facilities even though at the time around five thousand people were worshiping with them each weekend. Cordeiro replied, "We did a study of what it would cost to purchase our own worship space. If we did that, we would not be able to spend the amount of money we need to spend on leadership development." The odds are that New Hope may purchase facilities sometime in the distant future, but they have still set a precedent that is hard to ignore.

And what can we say about such influential churches like Bill Hybels's Willow Creek Community Church in Barrington, Illinois (www.willowcreek.org)? They spent their foundational years in rented movie theaters and are again renting meeting spaces for their expanding campuses. Or what about Saddleback Community Church (www.saddleback.com) in Lake Forest, California? That congregation shuffled between seventy-nine different places and reached more than ten thousand in regular attendance before erecting their first building. Legend is that it got to be a joke: people could attend, *if* they could find the church!

"I think we hold the record. We used 79 different locations during the first 15 years of the church. We grew to over 10,000 in attendance before we moved into our first permanent building in 1995—15 years after beginning. We often would use one location for Saturday night, a different one for Sunday morning, and a third location for midweek services. Since the schools we used

(5 different schools) were only available on weekends, literally everything else had to be held in businesses, warehouses, homes, restaurants, tents, parks, stadiums, other churches, theaters, etc."[8]
—Rick Warren, Pastor of Saddleback Church

Because of churches like New Hope, Willow Creek, Saddleback, and many other thriving congregations, the Nomadic Church is no longer viewed as a second-class way to do church. Christian leaders of the emerging world aren't as tied to property and space as are the leaders of earlier generations.[9] Many pastors are eager to take the gospel to the streets and don't have the money or patience for bricks and mortar. They're not willing to wait to tell the story, so the Nomadic Church is a Godsend to them—and the countless people they reach.

It's our belief that the percentage of churches renting facilities will continue to grow and that more and more churches will opt to rent nontraditional facilities as long as possible. If that's the case, more research needs to be done to learn how to fortify these mobile congregations.

Why the Nomadic Church?

In addition to what we've said, a serious case can be made for both the validity of the Nomadic Church and why the trend toward it is here to stay.

The New Testament church didn't need its own campus or special buildings, and neither do many of the rapidly growing ministries around the world. Even in the early church there were creative alternatives to permanent housing, like groups meeting in private homes, Paul renting the Lecture Hall of Tyrannus at Ephesus, and Justin Martyr holding classes for inquirers in a room over public baths.[10]

The early church responded to new situations and shifting needs by developing novel ministry approaches (see Acts 2:37-42;

15

6:1-6; 12:1-17; 13:1ff; 15:1ff). Astute leaders follow in their footsteps today.

According to the U.S. Census Bureau, $7.3 billion was spent on religious construction in 2000, up a hefty 89 percent from 1994.[11] Every year the cost of land and construction increases. To fulfill the Great Commission, the number of new churches that must be planted requires a method that demands less initial capital than in the past. When we ask denominational leaders why they aren't starting new churches, they inevitably mention their lack of money. But money is a major hindrance only if you're eager to buy land and construct a building. In talking with dozens of leaders in charge of church planting for their constituencies, we've learned that it costs between five hundred thousand and a million dollars to plant a church the traditional way![12]

With such an enormous price tag, it is impossible to plant the number of churches needed just to keep up with the population increase. The population growth of the U.S. is proportionately outstripping the number of churches. According to George Gallup in *Church in the World Today*, the church-to-population ratio is declining:

- In 1900, there were 27 churches for every 10,000 Americans.
- In 1950, there were 17 churches for every 10,000 Americans.
- In 1996, there were 11 churches for every 10,000 Americans.

Moreover, from 1986 to 1996 the combined membership of all Protestant denominations declined by 9.5 percent, while the national population increased by 11 percent.[13] It is, therefore, imperative that more effective churches are started in America—and as quickly and economically as possible!

Disadvantages of a Permanent Building

Many church planters eagerly await the day when they cut the ribbon on a new church facility. That desire is understandable and there certainly are benefits to a building. We're not trying to suggest otherwise. But it is equally important to consider advantages of the portable paradigm (see table 2) and disadvantages of owning a permanent church facility. Here are a few major drawbacks to owning church property that you need to be aware of.

- Cost—The capital needed to acquire land and then design, build, and maintain a permanent facility is astronomical. The closer you are to a population center, the higher the costs. And because land is a limited resource, its expense will only increase. Financial bondage is not uncommon for stationary churches.

- Focus—The massive amount of limited resources that must be expended on land and facilities may produce more lasting results—spiritually and eternally—if invested elsewhere. Buildings too easily drive and direct the energies of a church. As long as you can meet somewhere, purposefully putting your money into more people, programs, and pastors will out-produce funding a building any day.

- Limits—As much as buildings can initially boost a congregation's size, they can just as quickly limit it. Future growth is always limited by the present size of a facility, available parking, and zoning laws. In *When Not to Build*, Ray Bowman explains how church buildings can actually *kill* church growth.[14]

- Definition—Buildings can shape—or misshape—a church by communicating an inadequate image. Even the best designed building today can mis-define the essence or emphases of a church in a relatively short time. Then, you either suffer the consequences or go back to the drawing board and the money pit cycle.

- Affections—Church buildings can foster misplaced affections. They can produce unhealthy territorialism, a conviction that certain things ought never to be done in the building and certain others can be done only in the building, and even thinly veiled idolatrous building worship and ego stroking (consider the tower of Babel!). Sacred buildings are virtually universal in human religions, but Christianity does not require or endorse them—maybe for more reasons than meet the eye!

- Outreach—Perhaps Stuart Murray expresses this one best: "Having their own buildings may encourage churches to

17

operate with a centripetal ('come') rather than a centrifugal ('go') mentality in mission, inviting non-members on to church territory at times convenient to church members, rather than going into society to meet people on neutral territory, reversing the apparent thrust of mission in the New Testament."[15] Beyond that, the sheer volume of tax-free real estate owned by Christendom can turn off non-religious people, especially if they don't perceive the personal benefit of churches.

- Multiplication—Churches that have invested enormous amounts of money in buying land and building on it may warily view a proposal to use the building less in order to start a new church elsewhere. After all, redirecting financial assets may mean less ability to upkeep the present building. Mission can be minimized by maintenance.
- Effectiveness—A building can't solve nonbuilding problems, and mortar won't accomplish what ministry should accomplish. This is because buildings do not minister; only people do. Leaders too frequently expect a building to do things it never can—and they and their ministry suffer for it.

Churches that have learned to be effective without a permanent home are more likely not to be sucked into these pitfalls if and when they do build. That's why it is so critical to immerse a young congregation in a prudent, biblically balanced perspective on mission, people, buildings, service, and finances. It also helps for Nomadic Churches to know that it's not all rosy on the other side!

Advantages of the Nomadic Church

Despite many problematic issues and the amount of resources expended to respond to them, participants in our study indicate that there are scores of advantages to meeting in a rented facility. When we probed for specifics, interviewees quickly began giving several advantages (positives, pros, blessings) of being a Nomadic Church. Moreover, there were no qualifications of the advantages, like "that can be a plus, but . . ." Conversely, when discussing challenges, a person would sometimes chime in, "That can be hard, but there's a good side too . . ." Because of the importance of recognizing the positive aspects of the nomadic paradigm, we've provided a list of many of its advantages as perceived by various leaders we interviewed (see table 2). We often use their exact words so that you can hear directly from them. Use these thoughts to shape your own thinking about the benefits of mobile ministries.

Table 2: Advantages of the Nomadic Church Paradigm

Advantages to Being a Nomadic Church

- It forces creativity and flexibility.
- It permits time to build the church (people) before building the church building (bricks).
- It offers an irreplaceable experience of struggles and sacrifices; there is value in people "paying the price" for the church.
- It encourages people to trust God in unique ways and see God work in unique ways.
- It minimizes "clergy-laity" distinctions as all unite to make church "work."
- It attracts some previously churched people who have rebelled against church as an institution, of which buildings are a hallmark.
- It builds relational camaraderie, community, and intimacy within the congregation as a whole and within individual ministry teams.
- It means there is always something for everybody to do, and it challenges the "doers."
- It permits more focus on people, mission, and ministry.
- It lessens "fortress mentality," in which the church is viewed as a place to avoid and combat the world.
- It diminishes a centripetal ("come") mindset, while bolstering a centrifugal ("go") mindset.
- It surfaces congregants' "hidden" but useful talents, experience, passions, giftedness, and resources.
- It allows comparatively less traumatic transitions to larger/more adequate meeting facilities as needed or desired.
- It compels finding office space that is another adver-

tising and ministry forum in the actual target community.

- It opens up opportunities to minister to the host organization(s) and its personnel.
- It means the church will go to a new place and reach some they might not otherwise reach when they transition facilities.
- It teaches worship bands, drama teams, and the like how to take their mobile ministry outside of the church.
- It may force multiple worship services, which can offer more time and style options.
- It smothers idolatrous "building worship."
- It encourages purposeful (missional) budgeting, programming, planning, staffing, etc.
- It tends to be a more effective context for evangelism, as studies show people tend to come to Christ in greater numbers in newer churches.
- It provides leaders at all levels of the church with additional incentive to teach and model sacrificial stewardship.
- It keeps people praying.
- It has more of a "New Testament feel."
- It increases the value and effects of small group ministry.

- It lessens the chance that the church's image or mission is permanently shaped or mis-shaped by the building it meets in.
- It compels teamwork, unity, and interdependence.
- It builds humility because of not having a building and certain other "luxuries."
- It fosters a healthy sense of "ownership" of the church's mission and ministry.
- It engenders the virtue of patience due to long tenures as a Nomadic Church.
- It will make a future campus/building more meaningful.
- It forces decentralization into the community, thereby raising awareness of the church and facilitating interaction with the unreached.
- It fosters gratitude for the "simple things" (comfy chairs, clean carpets, cozy climate, etc.) and prevents taking them for granted.
- It draws some Christians who prefer a nonfacility-driven church or who want to be in on the "ground floor" of a newer church.
- It can provide a meeting site with plenty of meeting rooms, some educational equipment, a stage, theater-style seating, gyms, etc.

- It provides extra entry-level ministry opportunities (e.g., setup crew) to assimilate new attendees and equip them for additional ministry.
- It draws some who are wary of a "churchy" environment but less threatened by and more comfortable in a familiar public facility.
- It allows money and time that other churches spend on building maintenance, security, grounds upkeep, etc. to be put elsewhere.
- It can provide a site that is more visible to the community or more central to the target area than where a church could build.
- It keeps away some Christians who only want a "comfortable" church experience.
- It often forces advance planning (e.g., to contract a suitable meeting site), which gives more time to plan effective programs and events.
- It allows for faster multiplication of churches to saturate a city or area.
- It enlarges the value of hospitality and other home-based ministry.
- It builds a sense of corporate excitement and adventure.
- It encourages networking with other churches, which has multiple benefits.
- It permits faster adaptation of multi-campus and video venue paradigms.
- It develops attitudes and actions that will be invaluable if/when the church finally does build.

The Purpose of This Book

Despite the growing number of churches renting space for longer periods of time and in spite of the validity of their reasons for doing so, literature on the subject is slow to surface. Some of the more helpful resources are offered in appendix A. We feel that the lack of substantial and informative data contributes to the attrition rate of church plants in America and otherwise hinders the maximization of the ministry of Nomadic Churches.

Therefore, this book is an extensive reflection upon the challenges of the nomadic paradigm and various responses to them by experienced nomadic leaders. A major goal of our efforts is to harness and systematize knowledge from select successful

Nomadic Churches regarding challenges that can be traced to meeting in temporary facilities and ways in which nomadic leaders can address those challenges.

We confined the core of our research to multi-staffed churches that have been in existence for at least five years and have increased their worship attendance by over 500 percent. Moreover, they needed to be at *least* two hundred and fifty in average worship attendance and still renting space for corporate services. Beyond this, there is wide diversity among the participants. Our research was guided by one primary question— "What are the facility-related challenges faced by growing churches that rent temporary facilities on Sundays for corporate worship and other church functions, and how do they respond to them in order to continue growing and meet their stated ministry objectives?"

Our research methods included information forms and questionnaires, as well as on-site visits to multiple church services, interviews with a wide number of staff and lay leaders, and analysis of pertinent written material produced by leading Nomadic Churches. We also interacted with the limited relevant literature.

Finally, this work is bolstered by our personal experience consulting with and serving on the pastoral staffs of various Nomadic Churches. Admittedly, these years of experience mean that we bring some (largely positive) bias to our efforts. Yet we feel that even this "insider perspective" lends more credibility to our conclusions.

Together, we have compiled what we believe is the most useful information targeted toward churches housed in temporary locations. Enough common and coherent patterns emerged from our research to suggest that what follows is applicable to most, if not all, Nomadic Churches. We hope that knowing and applying this material will stimulate Nomadic Churches everywhere to maximize the fulfillment of their mission while minimizing expenditure of their limited resources. Read on to see for yourselves whether we've succeeded!

CHAPTER TWO

BIBLICAL TRUTH FOR THE NOMADIC CHURCH

Taking history as a whole, God's people have virtually always been a portable people by divine design and blessing. Even when the Lord ordained a stationary sanctuary—the *only* and *intentionally temporary* such structure—it was recognized by its very builders that the temple "cannot contain you" (1 Kgs 8:27), because "the God who made the world and everything in it is the Lord of heaven and earth, and does not live in temples built by hands" (Acts 17:24; cf. 7:33-54; 2 Chr 2:5-6; 6:18; Isa 66:1-2).[1] Rather than be preoccupied about the location of worship, Jesus assures us that "true worshipers will worship the Father in spirit and truth, for they are the kind of worshipers the Father seeks" (John 4:23).[2] Our nomadic God delights in nomadic worshipers!

"Genuine worship is spiritual. It is not dependent on places and things." —Leon Morris[3]

The only way to gain an understanding of the basic nature of the church—including its identity, practice, and place of worship—is by thoughtfully combing the pages of Scripture to extract its wealth of direct commands, historical examples, and valid principles. In this process we find that the Nomadic Church is not only biblical, but that it was foundational to the early church as well.

The goal of this chapter, however, is not to produce an ecclesiology, a theology of the corporate meeting place of God's people, nor any such grand endeavor. Our more modest objective is to show the biblical validity of the Nomadic Church and to illuminate key biblical guidance for our mobile ministries. Accordingly, nomadic leaders will be better equipped to respond to the inevitable questions: "When are we going to become a *real* church?" and "What does *God* say about how to make this thing work?"

The Early Church as Nomadic Church

When Nomadic pastors and planters look to Scripture for guidance concerning their particular ministry situation, they typically and appropriately look to the writings of the New Testament. After all, that's where the enriching story of the Church's Founder and foundation is recounted. It's there that we realize that Nomadic Churches are neither antithetical to God's nature nor an aberration from God's blueprint for the new covenant people. Edmund Clowney summarizes the New Testament perspective:

New Covenant worship . . . is free from the rituals of the Old Testament temple . . . God's presence was no longer localized at the temple in Jerusalem, but in Christ himself. . . . Worshippers do not look to a place on earth, because they look to where Jesus is. . . . [This] warns against our elaborating a form of worship that turns back to holy places.[4]

Today, no group of believers—no matter where they meet—can make special claim to the localized presence or glory of God, nor is any particular building or type of structure mandated as the "proper" place of worship. Jesus Christ is the personal fulfillment of the sacred tabernacle, temple, and their attendant services, since the whole old order was designed to be a shadow of the reality that was introduced and replaced by the new (John 2:19-20; Heb 8:1-10:10). Now, the dwelling of the omnipresent God with and within his people—regardless of their location—creates the only "sacred space" on earth (Acts 7:33-54; 17:24-29).

"For where two or three come together in my name, there am I with them." —Jesus Christ (Matthew 18:20)

Accordingly, local churches—like their first-century counterparts—are free to congregate wherever they can find suitable space to carry out their divine mission. Each of Christ's commissions and ordinances is people-focused rather than place-centered, and none require any particular meeting place (Matt 26:17-30; 28:18-20; Mark 16:15-18; Luke 24:44-49; John 20:21-23; Acts 1:4-8). Even the rare snapshots of a local church gathered in assembly (Acts 20; 1 Cor 14) demonstrate that Christians can corporately worship and "let all things be done for edification" (1 Cor 14:26 NKJV) without the aid of an ideal or specially constructed building.[5]

In many ways, including their portability and variety of "secular" meeting sites, the Nomadic Church actually looks *more* like the early church than do the many stationary churches of today!

Mobile churches are a completely legitimate expression of the universal *ekklesia* ("church"),[6] and Christians are living stones formed into the spiritual (not physical) temple of God (1 Cor 3:9, 16-17; 6:19; 2 Cor 6:16; 1 Pet 2:4-10). Any reading of the New Testament makes it clear that Nomadic Churches are neither spiritually disadvantaged nor inherently inferior to churches with their own buildings. In many ways, including their portability and variety of "secular" meeting sites,[7] the Nomadic Church actually looks *more* like the early church than do the many stationary churches of today!

Ultimately, the New Testament leads to the conclusion that since meeting facilities are a neutral tool to accomplish greater spiritual ends, they should not be a church's dominant preoccupation. Rather, *Whom* the church worships, *why* it meets, and *what* happens in assembly should be of exceedingly greater concern than *where* it happens.

With so many new churches returning to their nomadic New Testament roots, it's imperative to realize that Christianity has no special sanctuaries, churches have no sacred places, and God's presence has no spatial limitations.

Truth and Tips from the Tabernacle

In our zeal to probe the fertile New Testament revelation, we often overlook riches exposed by God's dealings with his even-more-ancient faith community. One such treasure for Nomadic Churches lies in the tabernacle narratives.

Although "the place [for worship] was not very important" up to and through the era of the patriarchs,[8] the mobility of God's people greatly intensified and formalized during the exodus from Egypt (Exod 12:31ff; Acts 7:36). During the exile the Lord instructed Moses: "Have [the Israelites] make a sanctuary for me, and I will dwell among them. Make this tabernacle and all its furnishings exactly like the pattern I will show you. . . . I will meet with you and give you all my commands for the Israelites" (Exod 25:8-9, 22; cf. Num 7:8-9).[9]

"The glory that resided above the ark in the Most Holy Place, to which the high priest had access once a year, is now walking the streets of Jerusalem for all to see, a truly portable tabernacle!" —Peter Enns[10]

The tabernacle represents the first of only two divine architectural blueprints for a physical worship structure. It deserves special attention, since it was the *only* time that the Lord ever gave instructions for a *portable* center of worship. Clearly, the tabernacle narratives were not intended to be a manual for nomadic ministry. But since *divine* wisdom ensured its success—despite the Israelites' inexperience with a mobile sanctuary—seeing how God alleviated their many portability challenges can unveil valuable insights for many of our facility-related challenges.

For starters, Nomadic churches should remember that Yahweh proactively designed the entire tabernacle to be a moveable worship center. It's evident from this—and in harmony with both Testaments—that God's nature doesn't demand that God's people be housed in a permanent building of splendor or comfort nor that the Lord be honored in such a setting. Being a nomadic people of God has unambiguous divine sanction in this and other periods of biblical history.

In the larger picture, the Lord established a detailed configuration for the tabernacle. Among other things, this allowed "setup workers" to know precisely how and where to arrange each item, saving valuable time, sparing needless confusion, and ensuring that nothing was overlooked. Providing workers with a schematic plot (facility layout) will similarly benefit Nomadic Churches, particularly for larger rental sites and larger congregations who need numerous workers or use rotating facility teams.

Beyond that, God's wisdom is seen in several tactical instructions that spared the Israelites certain problems related to their facility construction, setup, breakdown, and transportation. The provision for sturdy handles permanently attached to each major piece of furniture—the ark of the covenant, the table for the bread of the Presence, and the altars of burnt offering and incense—permitted quick and efficient movement of precious cargo while minimizing the chance of damage (see Exod 25:11-15, 26-28; 27:6-7; 30:4-5). Be they handles or rolling wheels with proper weight-bearing ratios, this strategy also increases a Nomadic Church's careful and timely transport of valuable items to and from storage space and transportation vehicles, as well as within rental sites.

It's noteworthy that rather than ordain many large furnishings, God opted to include only what was most strategic for fulfilling the tabernacle's purposes (i.e., items that reflected the Lord's

27

holiness and presence). This mission-driven and relatively light-weight design is beneficial when a worship center needs to be temporarily erected in the Sinai Desert or an American high school. However, the mobile design did not preclude elaborate ornate accessories that communicated spiritual meaning and contributed to the intended atmosphere.[11] Nomadic Churches also find that a little more space and time devoted to displaying spiritually meaningful and decorative objects greatly enhance the worship environment of any rental site.

Unlike most nomadic contexts, the entire structure of the tabernacle was designed to be portable. Still, the internal sectioning is of interest. Rather than constructing heavy walls, the Lord ordained the use of sturdy curtains to partition off "rooms" and sections (Exod 26:1-13; 36:8-17; cf. Heb 9:3).[12]

Thousands of years later, Nomadic Churches can also use comparatively lightweight curtains and other dividers to ease transportation struggles, create more usable space, make backdrops, enhance acoustics, provide relative privacy for groups, and accomplish multiple purposes in a large area that might otherwise be conducive to just one activity. When sturdy furnishings are desired (pulpit, soundboard, etc.), a church should consider taking the cue from the Lord's command to use "acacia wood" (mentioned twenty-five times in Exod 25–38). This extremely hard wood is known for its durability. As good stewards seeking to create an environment supportive of the church's mission, leaders should not purchase flimsy products when those items will serve important functions.

Related to the discussion of materials is the catalog of equipment God instituted. The Lord anticipated and specified all the essential supplies for the benefit of the inexperienced facility workers. Even comparatively small items played a valuable role in the spiritual and practical operation of the tabernacle (see Exod 25:29–27:19).

A Nomadic Church can also benefit from making and updating a master inventory list down to the smallest details. This can accelerate and better organize setup, breakdown, and transportation; provide a handy checklist for restocking and replacing items; and be used for budgeting and acquisition targets. As the Israelites did, this list can be used to assign people to be responsible for specific items and to ensure all supplies are accounted for and used appropriately.

Although the tabernacle's construction was principally managed by two divinely chosen and empowered men, Bezalel and Oholiab (Exod 31:1-11; 35:30-35; 36:1-2; 37:1ff; 38:22-23), the "whole Israelite community" was involved (Exod 35:1, 4). Moses implored: "All who are skilled among you are to come and make everything the LORD has commanded" (Exod 35:10), including "all the women who were willing and had the skill" (v. 26). The foremen were not to do all the work themselves because God gave "both [Bezalel] and Oholiab . . . the ability to teach others" (Exod 35:34). The outcome was that "the Israelites had done all the work just as the LORD had commanded" (Exod 39:42). They also amply funded it by a voluntary offering (Exod 25:2; 35:5, 21-29; 36:3-7), despite its enormous cost (cf. Exod 25:3-7; 35:5-9; 38:21-31).

Many people must also be integrally involved in the optimal funding, construction, and function of a modern Nomadic Church. It helps to identify a skilled person(s), whom we are calling "facility coordinators," to oversee facility-related affairs. Enlisting the help of a broad base of willing congregants makes the work proceed more quickly and efficiently. It also offers "entry-level" ministry opportunities and can breed a healthy sense of ownership and servanthood among those involved. This type of meaningful involvement in the church's operations also lends itself to greater generosity, as it did with the Israelites. This would alleviate some financial stresses newer churches inevitably face.

The Lord prescribed a well-organized division of labor and clear leadership roles for the tabernacle operations. Rather than recount it all here (see especially Num 3–4), figure 1 depicts this leadership configuration and how it could work out today. Organized, layered, and participatory leadership involving many trained people paid off then, as it does now!

Figure 1:
The Tabernacle Leadership Structure and a Contemporary
Configuration

God

Moses and Aaron
(Staff or Lay Facility Coordinators)

The Tribe of Levi
(The Facility Operations Team)

Eleazar and Ithamar
(Assistant Facility Coordinators)

Elizaphan, Eliasaph, and Zuriel
(Captains of Individual Facility Crews)

Kohathites, Gershonites, and Merarites
(Task-Specific Facility Crews)

Support by the Whole Israelite/Christian Community through
Special Skills, Voluntary Offerings, Etc.

Although there is a clear chain of command among the workers, that chain is joined with a sense of dignity, purpose, and
"team spirit." This approach to facility servants can generate
encouragement, longer service, easier recruiting, and higher
enthusiasm. It can also facilitate leadership development, which
is why churches like New Hope Christian Fellowship use the
position of "Levite" as one way to raise up future leaders.

The leaders and members of the tabernacle crews were given
their exact responsibilities and told specifically *how* to carry
them out.[13] Nothing was left to chance, and no one was unclear

about his role (e.g., Num 4:19, 27, 32, 49).[14] There was a healthy hint of holy paranoia!

The use of multiple facility crews with specific duties allows for specialized teams (e.g., audiovisual setup crew), wider workload distribution, higher accountability, and focused training. Having well-prepared teams with a manageable span of responsibility reduces burnout and increases retention, which by itself eases recruiting and training and makes the job more purposeful and enjoyable. The resulting environment can enhance rather than detract from the church's spiritually significant activities each Sunday.

Nomadic Churches will find it beneficial to follow our Lord's proactive appointing of qualified leaders to oversee specified facility-related tasks. As the size, needs, and desired quality of a church increase, so should the layers of leadership, number of leaders, and teams they oversee. Each team and leader will be strengthened by having a written job description to follow, which can also help with evaluation. Similarly, helpers can more proficiently fulfill their assigned duties when written operating policies and procedures are established and consistently followed. That's certainly why the Lord initiated such tools for the Israelites.

When each person understands his or her specific tasks, there will be increased efficiency and reduced confusion. Knowing what specific roles need to be filled can help leaders strategically place new recruits and, thus, have more continuity on facility crews. Rather than becoming a drain on the church or a detriment to its mission, the facility can serve as a strategic tool for ministry. After all, that's why facilities are there!

CHAPTER THREE

CHALLENGES FACING THE NOMADIC CHURCH

Ideal conditions for ministry rarely, if ever, exist. The incipient church in Acts quickly grew to understand that reality.[1] The problems modern American churches face generally pale in comparison to past and present trials encountered amid the advance of Christianity around the globe. Yet legitimate challenges do indeed exist for local churches—including nomadic ones. And for effective ministry to flourish, those challenges must be understood and addressed.

Nomadic Churches have essentially all of the same challenges faced by churches who own their property. But beyond the normal stresses and struggles of ministry are complications that arise from renting meeting and office facilities and having to cart enormous amounts of equipment from place to place each week and turn an otherwise sterile environment into the setting for a worshipful experience. As we shall see, there are many less apparent problems too.

From our research we discovered that Nomadic Churches are confronted with six categories of facility-related challenges: (1) physical, (2) program, (3) personnel, (4) visitor, (5) special events, and (6) financial. Within these categories are countless individual issues and themes, many of which we will surface in the following chapters.

We use the phrase "facility-related challenge" to refer to any mild to severe limitation, burden, inconvenience, difficulty, stress, hazard, or hardship that is directly or indirectly traceable to being a Nomadic Church that holds services in a temporary, rented facility over an extended period of time.

Figure 2 shows the approximate frequency and severity these groupings of challenges have in the everyday life of the Nomadic Churches that took part in our research.

Figure 2

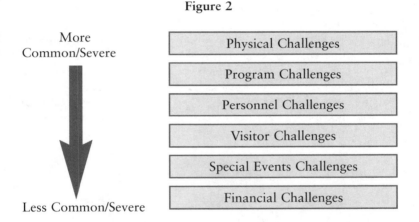

More Common/Severe

Less Common/Severe

Physical Challenges

Program Challenges

Personnel Challenges

Visitor Challenges

Special Events Challenges

Financial Challenges

The order of these challenges presents a logical flow. The broadest and most severe category—physical challenges—leads to numerous programmatic challenges. Many facility personnel must be deployed to combat them. Moreover, what affects programs often affects special events, which occur less frequently than ongoing programs and so are ranked as slightly less common/severe. The same physical challenges that have an impact on programs and special events have the tendency to determine, at least partly, whether certain people will visit or remain at a church. Finally, certain financial expenses are incurred to alleviate or prevent these challenges.

Thematic Overlap

Problems rarely stand alone. During our study it became apparent that many facility-related issues have more than one source and consequence. Take the exasperating example of a school custodian who fails to show up on time to unlock the school doors for a church. By being late, all the setup is pushed back. Facility volunteers face inconvenience. Some routine modifications to the meeting site may remain undone for lack of time. Setup and worship practice become rushed. Chaos threatens the children's classes, and programs run short. Something that morning might bother an uncommitted visitor enough to prevent his or her return to the church. Rent paid for the unused facility time may not be reimbursed, or one of many other consequences could ensue. Thus, the "physical challenge" of locked doors could also fairly be viewed as a program, personnel, visitor, and financial challenge—even a special events challenge, if an event or event practice was scheduled that day. There are many other examples of how multiple categories of challenges and themes within categories intersect (figure 3).

Figure 3:
Thematic Overlap

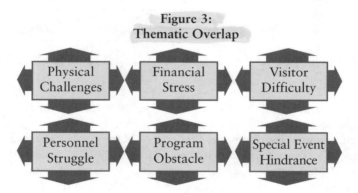

The web represented in figure 3 could be drawn in any number of ways, depending on the issue under discussion. It helps explain why we mention some issues in more than one category of challenges, and why we do not elaborate on every issue within each category. Whenever an issue is raised in the following chapters, why not ask yourself: "What other challenges could result from this one? Could it put an additional strain on our workers? Could it cause an obstacle to one of our programs? Could it limit a special event we've wanted to do? Could it present a barrier to attracting or retaining a visitor? Could it add another financial burden?" By looking at issues in this interconnected way, successful nomadic leaders train themselves to anticipate and prevent problems that might otherwise blindside them.

In the context of this book, a "response" refers to how Nomadic Church leaders intuitively or intentionally prevent or constructively react to a particular facility-related challenge or set of challenges, whether in their thinking, attitudes, or actions.

We'll examine each of these groups of facility-related challenges as well as how successful Nomadic Churches have learned to respond to them so that their corporate goals are not compromised. More established Nomadic Churches may wish to skim the chapters that discuss the facility-related challenges (chapters 4, 6, and 8), although an awareness of the issues other Nomadic Churches face can still be helpful. After all, the next facility move will very likely present some new challenges even experienced churches haven't yet faced. Whether you're about to launch a Nomadic Church or are serving an established one, two sets of discussion questions are provided at the end of the following chapters to help you process and apply the material with your key leaders. (Feel free to e-mail us your responses to these questions at Easum@easumbandy.com.)

Stay with us; it may spare you the headache of learning some very valuable lessons the hard way.

CHAPTER FOUR

REVEALING PHYSICAL AND PERSONNEL CHALLENGES

Among the most pressing categories of facility-related challenges encountered by even highly effective Nomadic Churches are physical and personnel challenges. An examination of appendix A shows that they also emerge as major topics in the literature, as well as sporadically in the biblical record. Every church has some physical and personnel challenges, but the ones we'll examine arise from being a portable church.

Physical and personnel challenges refer to mild to acute problems, limitations, or stresses that a Nomadic Church faces related to physical, material matters concerning the meeting facility and the people directly involved with its operations.

Several themes of physical and personnel challenges emerged in our research. Each entry in table 3 represents a set of interrelated issues within these broader categories. As we learned in the previous chapter, many of these themes and the issues within them intersect each other and one or more of the other categories of challenges (figure 3). Accordingly, some of them will surface later, although many are considered here because of their direct relationship to the categories of physical and personnel challenges.

Table 3: Themes Within Facility-related Physical Challenges

Storage Shortages	Aesthetic Irritations	Display Difficulties	Odorous Distractions	Parking Problems
Host-Tenant Strains	Transportation Trials	Legal Alarms	Security Anxieties	Construction Obstacles
Setup/Break-down Toil	Comfort Deficit	Retaining Stresses	Audiovisual Limitations	Climate Controls
Space Restrictions	Privacy Barriers	Training Troubles	Recruiting Resistance	Facility Relocations

For discussion purposes, the themes are grouped together into three larger subcategories of physical and personnel challenges to which they best relate: (1) setup/breakdown struggles, (2) atmospheric stresses, and (3) host-tenant strains. Since the majority of Nomadic Churches rent space in school buildings, many examples involve that context. Still, this information is applicable to a wide range of meeting sites, because the churches we studied have also utilized space ranging from movie theaters and community centers to firehouses and funeral homes. Not every issue or theme applies to every church or meeting site at all times. But beware: If you haven't run across these bumps, they may lie right around the corner!

Setup/Breakdown Struggles

Among the most persistent challenges faced by Nomadic Churches are recruiting, training, retaining, and managing servant (volunteer) facility workers, storing and transporting church equipment, manipulating the meeting site to make it conducive to the church's activities, and the actual setting up and breaking down of the many items brought to and from the facility. So much of a church's ability to focus on its spiritual priorities depends on the facility workers who handle these matters. Mark Stephens, executive pastor of Seneca Creek Community Church, commented while watching several people roll out large carpets and set up equipment for a packed children's program, "If it wasn't for them, we couldn't pull this off."

"For us in the early hotel years, it [the hard part] was getting the teams to move the equipment each Sunday morning and setting up a 'rock concert' sound system and children's ministry rooms, when everyone would rather have been sleeping in a few extra hours." — Ken Okajima, Director of Operations, NewSong Church, Irvine, California (www.newsong.net)

"Them" is usually a relatively small group who function as the setup/breakdown team. On any given Sunday, they work longer and harder—at least in a physical sense—than anyone else in the church. (Okay, the junior high boys' teacher may be the lone exception!) A few "lucky" ones forfeit their Saturday nights to prepare the facility for services the next day. Most, however, arise in the dark Sunday morning hours to engage in their ritual of "unseen sacrifice," as one associate pastor put it. It is precisely because of these people's Christlike servant attitude, which repeatedly surfaced in our conversations with nomadic leaders, that we usually prefer to use the term "servant" instead of "volunteer" to refer to these people.

Elwin Ahu used to be a circuit court judge. When he became a Christian his assignment as a Levite at New Hope Christian Fellowship was to scrub the toilets at the ministry center, which he often spent hours doing alone in the middle of the night. He is now the executive pastor.

Once breakdown is done, the facility reset, and church belongings returned to storage, it may be late in the afternoon. The length of time depends on the number of helpers and the distance of the storage site(s). And depending on the frequency of evening and midweek gatherings, the cycle of being "on the road again" can seem endless.

A typical Sunday morning involves loading an assortment of items from wherever they are stored—usually off-site in warehouses, converted vans or trailers, participants' homes, office suites, rented storage garages, or any other available space that can be claimed. Depending on the number and capacity of transport vehicles, this can necessitate two or more round-trips each Sunday. It may also mean repeatedly wrestling heavy equipment and bulky loads over curbs and up and down stairs and loading ramps. Throw some inclement weather in the mix, and the whole process gets a bit more hectic.

Although teachers, musicians, greeters, and others typically have to transport armloads of supplies in their own vehicles each Sunday, the churches without on-site storage (which is most of them!) bring the bulk of the equipment in designated vehicles. If you stand outside most Nomadic Churches one to two hours before the first program is scheduled to start, you'll see an unorganized parade of cars, trucks, vans, and SUVs doing their "drop off duty." The most fortunate churches tow large transport trailers behind trucks, but training people to drive these "monsters" (as one assistant facility coordinator called them) and back into tight spots for loading and unloading is "nerve-racking." Even *finding* willing drivers can be a headache—one made worse if the type of vehicle requires its operator to have a commercial license.

Once on site, servants with carts, crates, and cabinets scatter in every direction to unload their cargo. Dozens of people spend an average of two hours, excluding travel, transforming some aspect of the facility. They often follow mostly unwritten policies, and they grow wiser with experience. In the absence of formalized training programs like those that teachers, greeters, and others often enjoy, there is virtually always at least one "green" facility helper learning the job alongside a more experienced servant. After all, this kind of training can't be done in a classroom.

"It takes excruciating energy to set up and tear down." —Rob Winkler, Senior Pastor of Turning Point Christian Center, Vancouver, Washington (www.turningpointcc.org)

Unleashing the church-in-a-box involves setting up a seemingly endless list of essential equipment that a stationary church might easily take for granted: sound systems, speakers, staging, video projectors, portable screens, musical instruments, risers, pulpits, Christian education supplies, lights, folding chairs, meeting tables, sign-in stations, drama sets, carpets, clocks, curtains and dividers, communion tables, banners, plants, literature kiosks, refreshment centers, resource carts, information booths, and more. Adding to the strain is that some of these items must be set up in *several* places for the different ministries spread throughout the facility. We observed people at one church assemble six separate projection systems for different groups. At New Hope in Oahu, an overflow room requires setting up extremely large projection systems for crowds up to six hundred in number.

In addition, people engage in various aspects of assembling nursery areas, arranging multiple classrooms, posting internal and external directional signs, and making many other facility enhancements. Since some sites are regularly dirty and cluttered when the facility crew arrives (movie theaters are among the worst offenders), a few busy themselves vacuuming, mopping, picking up trash, wiping down sinks, and doing other forms of cleaning. The longer it takes to complete their tasks, the more the church has to pay for the space and the harder it is to attract new helpers.

"Everything we do is volunteer intensive. The routine wears on workers and equipment alike." —Greg St. Cyr, Senior Pastor of Bay Area Community Church, Annapolis, Maryland (www.bayareacc.org)

40

It's almost a joke at some Nomadic Churches: You can tell who's on the facility crew by the sweat on their foreheads. Because of the demands, replacements don't eagerly "line up" to cover for them. Especially when the church is newer, most facility workers are part of the faithful core who fill more than one ministry role. Later on, some churches find it necessary to pay a facility coordinator in order to keep someone in the demanding position of overseeing this whole process each week.

When we inquired about the average tenure of a setup/breakdown worker, one facility coordinator told us with a wink, "Until they burn out!" He further noted, "There's usually a new guy to train." Perhaps this issue can best be summarized by one written response to our question about how many people assist in setup and breakdown: "Too few. This is an ongoing challenge!"

Atmospheric Stresses

No matter how suitable a particular rental site is, it invariably has shortcomings in comparison with the relative luxury offered by a modern church facility. Those deficiencies can often be traced to atmospheric stresses, which represent an assortment of inconveniences, struggles, and obstacles imposed by aspects of the atmosphere, environment, or configuration of the rental site. With a mixture of guidance from senior leadership, help from other ministry volunteers, and personal ingenuity, the same facility workers described above are also on the frontline of the battle to prevent and alleviate these stresses. We've isolated a few standouts.

Parking Problems

Parking repeatedly surfaces as a problem. It's no minor issue either, because if people can't park, they can't attend! High schools, theaters, college campuses, and the like generally have sufficient parking. However, churches meeting in places like elementary schools, private residences, and daycare centers face the largest shortage since these places don't need many parking spaces during the week.

It takes extra effort each week to reserve specially designated spots where guests can park. During winter weather, parking lots may not be cleared of snow, especially if the host has no need to open the doors to its regular constituency on Sunday. Having a member with a snowplow is "golden" in these situations, said one facility coordinator.

Then there is the occasional "surprise event" scheduled on a Sunday in part of a school or on its activity fields. The parking lot that was already barely large enough to support the church can suddenly be overcrowded. More annoying yet, parking lots need periodic repaving, and the weekend is the best time for the school to do it. It is when these kinds of "Sunday morning crises" hit that nomadic pastors are more likely to hear people grumble, "Pastor, when are we going to become a *real* church?"

Physical Repairs

Most churches schedule their maintenance, repairs, and upgrades on weekdays when their building is less used. But for the same reasons, school administrators and property managers prefer to have these tasks performed on the weekends. Schools reserve longer projects for the summer—or for two of the busiest times on the Christian calendar: Christmas (winter break) and Easter (spring break). At least this makes the holidays "extra eventful," as one worship leader put it.

Another example of inconvenience is roof repairs. If this does not close the building altogether, it means moving classes or services to a less optimal place (e.g., from a school auditorium to its cafeteria or library). This is not as simple as it may sound, given the numerous logistical issues involved in creating a suitable worship center. Plus, the stench from the tar being applied to the roof can be overwhelming enough to drive some people away.

Because of liability concerns, some organizations dislike or forbid having a church in their facility during any period of construction. Many of the pains we've mentioned pale in comparison to the sting of being told that renovations will close the meeting site altogether for a time. Such news sends church leaders on a mad scramble to find another suitable place to meet. Rarely do they end up with something as desirable as the place they previously rented, or else they would already be meeting there. In one case, county officials scheduled massive repairs to take place in *all* their older schools during the summer. Not only did that mean Occoquan Bible Church (www.obc.org) in Woodbridge, Virginia, had to find a place to meet, it also meant they had to "compete" with numerous other displaced churches.

Cleaning Time

Nomadic Churches eagerly welcome the extra cleaning efforts of their hosts. Unfortunately, these efforts often happen on the weekends. Not every pastor has the pleasure of walking into the church building to find that a new custodial worker chose to wax and then block off entire hallways the night before! The annual pre-school cleaning—an intense period of facility preparation for a new school year—presents its own set of hassles. A church can figure on playing "musical rooms" during this month as parts of the facility they normally use are shut down and rearranged into different configurations.

Even if overcrowded rooms aren't an acute problem most of the time, the "cleaning season" can overcrowd even the most spacious facility when not enough suitable space is available elsewhere in the building.

One might deal better with the inconveniences during this period if they were simply a manifestation of the school's obsession with cleanliness. But stained carpets, food spills, dirty bathrooms (with little to no soap and toilet paper), sticky seats, stinky lockers, scattered trash, burned out lights, and sometimes worse conditions are a familiar part of the nomadic experience.

Climate Control

At some sites church leaders are denied access to the climate controls. This is particularly true of schools and places that have several buildings governed by one thermostat. Unless a responsible host representative sets the thermostat to a comfortable degree sufficiently early, a pleasant temperature is often not attained until morning activities are well under way, if at all. One exasperated leader explained to us on a chilly morning that in some schools (like his) there is no ability to modify the thermostat from inside the school. They must rely on a central office— one that tries to save money on weekend heating and cooling. They don't rush to fix power outages on the weekend either, so Sundays without electricity tend to send Nomadic Churches back to the "Dark Ages."

Needing to keep the doors open so long for setup, for people to enter the facility, and then for teardown doesn't help the situation. This is especially problematic in places where the "sanctuary doors" are located close to the main entrance. Sitting on the metal folding chairs that some Nomadic Churches have to use only intensifies the cool temperatures. Even more distressing is when schools fail to fix air-conditioning problems in the summer or heating problems in the winter when school is out.

One Size Doesn't Fit All

Daycare centers and elementary schools present their own set of problems. From coat racks to water fountains to tiny tables, just about everything is designed for small children. Bathrooms are a good example. They are not only too small, but seldom are there enough for adults. The few more suitable teacher facilities can be located well away from areas the church actually uses and are sometimes declared "off limits."

One size does not fit all ages, but many Nomadic Churches are presently constrained to use a "one-size-fits-all" facility.

The converse is also true. Movie theater and high school furnishings are often unsuitable for children, and churches have to bring and arrange *small* tables and chairs for their younger children's classes. Nurseries are a story unto themselves. Churches that don't make the furnishings fit the person can expect to pay the price in attendee losses.

Distractions

When asked about the drawbacks to being a Nomadic Church, pastors regularly mention the diversity of distractions in their meeting sites. Jeff Carroll, pastor of Trinity Community Church (www.trinitycc.org), in Bowie, Maryland, notes: "There is a certain level of distraction that can compete for the attention of the people because the room is not designed for worship." Distractions range from poor acoustics and lighting, to broken and blowing window blinds, to accidentally crushed communion cups on the floor. "Busy" painted murals on the walls, prominently displayed school logos, and student art-work hung all around the makeshift "sanctuary" introduce their own diversions. There are only so many jokes you can make when the configuration of a gym forces the preacher to speak underneath a basketball hoop. Chairs are sometimes warped or broken, and some are notoriously squeaky. At least that noise is better than the echoes endured by the classes that meet in the racquetball courts of fitness centers!

Meeting in a public facility designed for a certain age range introduces other environmental distractions. Halloween can be a hectic time because of the "festive" decorations displayed at some sites. Then there are the movie theater advertisements that puzzle young children and make moms hurry them down the hall. A Christian education director told us that before a teacher could catch what happened, a class of young children was exposed to a graphic drawing of a naked man and woman in the health classroom of a middle school. Consider part of an e-mail written to a pastor by the children's director at Seneca Creek Community Church:

> Matthew (age 9, 3rd grade) has always loved our church very much. This morning as [he and his mother, Leslie] pulled up to church he said he didn't think they should come to this church anymore. Leslie asked him why and he told her, "They believe that Athena (and other Greek gods) are gods." He said this because he had seen pictures of the Greek gods somewhere in Seneca Valley High School. Leslie was able to explain to him so he was okay, but it makes me wonder how many other children have wondered about this or something else they have seen in their church environment and haven't said anything. Leslie said that last year there was a little girl in her class that was upset by a mask that was on the wall that looked mean—she thought it was Jesus.[1]

45

The dilemmas created by subtle—and not so subtle—distractions are rarely just innocent annoyances. Without proactive intervention, they can be downright counterproductive to the mission of Christ's church.

Privacy Issues

Most churches probably don't give matters of privacy a second thought, but Nomadic Churches have special challenges in this area. The offices and unused areas of the meeting site are typically locked. Parents may struggle to find an isolated place to discipline their child, if needed. No pastoral or administrative offices exist for a quick conversation with a member. Emergency leadership meetings have to be held at the end of a hall or in the corner of a lobby, barely out of listening range.

Space is also limited for the inevitable "crisis counseling" or evangelistic follow-up that presents itself some Sunday mornings. A special "cry room" for nursing mothers is seldom possible. The lack of doors on many school bathroom stalls, which one custodian explained were removed "for safety reasons," is also a major problem for many adults. These issues, while not insurmountable, seem largely unique to Nomadic Churches and make for some complicated situations.

Host-Tenant Strains

Most pastors feel strongly that their churches have worked hard to have a good relationship with their host(s). Nevertheless just about every church has (or will have!) one or more "horror stories" about a struggle with its leasing agent.[2]

A Nomadic Church "is essentially at the mercy of its rental facility's owner. . . . It makes us live by faith every day." —Ed Doepel, Senior Pastor of Crossroads Community Church, Naperville, Illinois (www.ccc4christ.net)[3]

This is no trivial matter. Several churches we've studied have actually left or been forced to leave a site because of a breakdown in this relationship. We've mentioned some strains, like careless climates and storage stinginess. We'll spare you the juicy stories, but here are some other issues we've run across.

Unfair Accusations

"War language" is sometimes used. Unhappy notes left on lecterns, desk drawers conspicuously taped shut, and cryptic messages scrawled on chalkboards let church workers know they are "intruding" on another's territory. Some teachers "seem to have a mission to get us kicked out," reported one Christian education director. A pastor at another church described the relationship with the school as "an ongoing battle." We've been told of repeated accusations of damage, theft, and even killing classroom pets. When things *are* legitimately damaged or disorganized by church members, it only perpetuates the misgivings. Compounding the strain is school management's tendency not to give prior notice of various inconveniences that will occur on a given Sunday. "Sometimes we just show up and find out about a problem," reported more than one facility coordinator.

Part of the tension stems from individual schools receiving very little benefit from leasing their space to an outside group. Usually, the rent money goes directly into the county school system rather than into the school's own accounts. When teachers or janitors complain, the administration may be unenthusiastic about defending the rights of the "weekend invaders."

Custodial Problems

Those with whom churches in schools most directly and frequently interact are the custodial staff. Janitors literally hold the keys to making the morning experience miserable or manageable, and they exercise that power for better or worse.

Some simply "forget" to open up the school or to find a replacement when they're sick or out of town. Others wait to clean the facility until *after* the church leaves. Then there are those who refuse to go to the school to open it up if there is even a hint of inclement weather, much to the dismay of the powerless

47

pastor. While a church *may* be excused from paying for this lost time, it may not be able to make up what was lost in giving or growing. At other critical times, no custodian can be found to remedy a situation that only he or she can fix. That's especially frustrating since the contract typically requires them to stay on the premises for the express purpose of troubleshooting facility issues that arise. More than one church discovered the custodian was "out for breakfast" when he or she was needed most.

Legal Concerns

Legal concerns sometimes make matters worse between the church and the host.

Despite Supreme Court rulings to the contrary, modern misunderstandings of "separation of church and state" have made some organizations wary of having churches meet on their property.

High publicity cases keep churches and hosts alike on edge. Some school officials and teachers have let occupants know of their legal misgivings with having a church in their quarters. Legal concerns meld into the power of the school system or city hall manager to terminate a rental contract. It's no surprise that one pastor told us, "[Legal concerns] always stay in the back of my mind."

The threat of eviction can turn into an enormous anxiety. Although the length can vary based on many factors, renting one place for the duration of the nomadic experience is exceptionally rare.[4] While most transitions are voluntary moves, some churches are forced out.

One church reported that they were left with no legal recourse when every public school in their county was closed for the summer, spring break, and winter break periods. An outreach pastor shared his experience of initially being excluded from renting property in a public park because of the church's religious status, while another church gave up on trying to meet in their city hall after months of resistance. One pastor shared, "There's always a fear that our contract won't be renewed." Perhaps he was concerned because the church's first school ended their contract simply "because janitors didn't want to work anymore on weekends." A county school official even told him that there are already too many churches in schools. In some counties a church is technically not supposed to rent a school for more than two years. At a minimum, they must present evidence that they do not plan to be a "permanent resident."

Beyond this resistance lies the issue of churches being charged a higher rental rate than other outside groups. Schools and other government facilities have tried to justify this illegal practice in many ways. Fortunately, a lawyer's letter can usually resolve that issue quickly, though it may never heal the resulting fracture between church and host. If it's not somehow repaired, however, the church may all too quickly find itself on the road again.

Talk Time for Teams

For Pre-Plant Teams

- After reading this chapter, what have you learned to be aware of that you may not have considered before?

- How does this information influence what kind of rental facility you seek to secure for church services? What questions will you want to ask potential hosts before you settle on a site (also look under "Whitson" in appendix A)?

- How does this chapter shape your attitude toward your launch team members?

- Does reading this material cause you to view the overall mobile experience any differently than you did before? How?

- What does this chapter imply about your reliance upon and faith in God? In each other?

For Post-Plant Teams

- Can you identify with the challenges described in this chapter? If so, which ones? Share your stories and perspectives with each other.

- What other examples of facility-related physical and personnel challenges could you add to what's presented in this chapter?

- How do this chapter and your discussion affect your thoughts, feelings, attitudes, values, and actions toward:
  God,
  your meeting site,
  your leaders,
  your ministry volunteers,
  your community, and
  your rental host?

CHAPTER FIVE

RESPONDING TO PHYSICAL AND PERSONNEL CHALLENGES

The effective Nomadic Church stubbornly refuses to allow space to determine mission. Instead, it finds ways to minimize, if not eliminate, the challenges presented by its physical surroundings. While some think there are things a mobile congregation simply can't do, the churches we've studied prove that the lack of a building doesn't have to translate into a lack of ministry. The quality and quantity of what many Nomadic Churches do is impressive by any standard!

"We have yet to find a ministry function that cannot be done excellently in a rented facility." —Pete van der Harst, founder and president of Portable Church Industries (www.portablechurch.com), and Dana Cadman[1]

Our goal in this chapter is to share some ways successful Nomadic Churches cope with their physical and personnel challenges. The responses are grouped into the same three subcategories offered in the previous chapter—setup/breakdown struggles, atmospheric stresses, and host-tenant tensions. This discussion will be noticeably longer than the others because responses to these challenges are foundational to relieving many other facility-induced shortcomings that we'll see later.

Responses to Setup/Breakdown Struggles

The setup/breakdown struggles we previously identified relate to:

- Recruiting, training, retaining, and managing volunteer facility workers;
- Storing and transporting church equipment;
- Manipulating the meeting site to make it conducive to the church's activities (also considered in later chapters); and
- The actual setting up and breaking down of items brought to and from the facility.

The negative effects of these persistent challenges, along with some we will expose later, can be prevented or greatly minimized through implementing preventative and tactical measures that align with the following categories:

• Teamwork	• Support Systems
• Organization	• Encouragement
• Portability	• Consultation

Let's take a closer look at each of these.

Teamwork

Every church we surveyed identified teamwork as integral to preventing and responding to facility-related challenges.[2] Teams allow church leaders to break the workload into manageable pieces and establish a workable span of care. This prevents meltdown over the long haul, endows facility workers with a greater sense of purposefulness, makes it far easier to recruit new servants, and fosters fun and fellowship.

No growing Nomadic Church expects just a few people to handle all that goes into transforming the facility from a generic site into one serviceable for the church.

At least three basic teams are integral to every Nomadic Church:

- A *media team* that focuses on audiovisual matters;
- A *"front door" team* that tends to welcoming and first impression matters like aesthetic touches, signs, refreshment center(s), and church information tables; and
- A general *setup/breakdown team* that transports, unloads, arranges, and performs other facility preparation and departure matters.

Task-specific crews are multiplied as the size of the church and complexity of its activities expand. One that is often overlooked is a "decision team," which helps people register spiritual decisions made during the morning. In smaller churches, this can be part of the duties of the "front door team."[3] Many Nomadic Churches ask every person who commits to membership to help with some aspect of facility operations as a "community contribution" in addition to their other areas of service. At least one church actually circulates a list of ongoing and occasional facility-related service opportunities for people to sign up for at the conclusion of their membership course.

Beyond the essential teams, individual ministries often assume responsibility to arrange their own functional space and pack up their belongings at the end of the last service. Youth ministries sometimes have "mini-teams" who focus on facility matters specific to their programs. Teachers typically prepare their own classroom for the morning activities. In larger churches, it is more likely to see facility crews arrange the rooms and prepare large group meeting areas. Walkie-talkies help them work as a unit to coordinate their efforts and waste less time running back and forth to exchange messages.

To recruit enough facility workers, it is paramount to hold the position in as high esteem as any other ministry role and to promote the available service opportunities in every conceivable way.

One church we studied experienced the burnout of two consecutive nursery directors. When the family pastor figured out it was because the directors were trying to do everything by themselves, he implemented a system with four "weekly supervisors" who rotate the setup/breakdown responsibilities. The director only covers the extra weekend in months with five weeks. "Most people can handle it if it's not every week," said the most recent (and most content!) nursery director.

There is at least one notable distinction between setup and breakdown. Virtually every church we interviewed says it takes nearly twice as long to set up the meeting site as to break it down. The reason: Many more people are on site at the conclusion of services than early in the morning before they begin. Alert leaders take advantage of the presence of these "extras" by soliciting their help for breakdown and inviting them to help with setup the next week.

Some responsibilities are rotated within the setup teams themselves. At Bay Area Community Church a team of six rotates picking up the transport trucks and being responsible for setup, breakdown, and returning the trucks. In this system, nobody carries the greatest load more than two months a year. Northstar Church (http://northstarpc.org) in Panama City, Florida, uses its small group ministries to handle the setup operations. Interestingly, Northstar is one of the few churches that told us it has little problem securing setup and breakdown crews. These team-based tactics distribute the tremendous Sunday workload among many people so that it is more manageable than if it were to fall on just a few shoulders.

Facility teams should not be comprised only of the muscle men in the church. Women can participate in setup functions, especially if you design your equipment to be lightweight and mobile (see below). Teens can pitch in, too. A core value of Occoquan Bible Church is "Families Serving Together." So, while observing this church in action, we were not surprised at how many family units pitched in to help. Fathers and sons worked together on the setup/breakdown crews, and even preschoolers helped Mom and Dad carry smaller items down the hall to the awaiting transportation. Many congregations have discovered that family involvement is but one of the hidden joys of renting space.

A few Nomadic churches bypass some setup/breakdown struggles by deploying their teams on Saturday evenings to prepare the facility for Sunday services. Although this usually incurs extra rental costs, it can ease Sunday morning chaos, allow time to untangle last minute snags, promote more interaction with guests, and include helpers who are preoccupied with other duties on Sunday. Even the extra rental costs can be negated (see chapter 9). It's an option worth exploring, particularly for large churches, those with an early Sunday morning service, or those who need to do extensive adjustments to make the site ready for services.

Organization

Every Nomadic Church should have an organizational structure that ensures needs are met, ministry is taking place, and burnout is avoided. Organization is so important that Seneca Creek Community Church includes it among its "Ten Keys to Building a Truly Great Church." Don't assume everyone instinctively knows what, when, and how to carry out facility operations, and don't make them learn the hard way. Many churches provide their servants with written policies that are periodically evaluated and modified based on their growing experience, equipment upgrades, and changing meeting site.

Rather than rely on memories or settle for mediocrity, we've found that the more efficient Nomadic Churches engage in at least the following organizational activities:

• Compile a complete checklist of every material thing you will need to set up and take down. An excellent free sample is provided at Passion for Church Planting's Web site at http://www.church-planting.net. Just click on the "Free Church Planting Resources."

- Write simple, short, specific, and measurable ministry descriptions for every position.

- Interview prospective facility crew leaders and helpers to ensure that they are a good match and understand the duties of their respective position.

- Follow a training procedure for each facility recruit, however informal it may be.

- Enforce clear lines of responsibility so that every worker knows who to ask help from or report a problem to.

- Maintain an updated list of alternate servants in case of emergencies.

- Assign the same qualified people to handle certain skilled tasks for maximum efficiency and excellence (e.g., sound system setup).

- Divide responsibilities among various task-specific crews (see earlier examples), and make sure no one person or group carries an unreasonable load or never gets a break.

- Develop a "quality control checklist" to simplify setup and breakdown and ensure nothing is left undone or behind.

- Establish an optimal order for items to be loaded onto and off of transportation vehicles. This ensures equal weight distribution and maximal use of space within vehicles.

- Prioritize the order in which setup needs to be done (e.g., outdoor signs posted, thermostat adjusted, coffee started, carpets laid).

- Label storage boxes and equipment clearly so that helpers know what's inside the containers and where they go without having to open each one.

- Post diagrams of the facility and room arrangements so that workers know exactly where to take church belongings in the site, how to set them up, and how to reconfigure rooms after services.

- Update the rental contract as soon as changes occur.

- Implement careful record keeping (e.g., bill payment schedule) for all matters that involve the host.

Our surveys revealed a conspicuous trend: The less setup/breakdown organization a church has and the less training it does, the harder it is for leaders to recruit and retain facility servants.

These and other organizational measures permit new facility workers to be immediately plugged into the setup system without lengthy tutorials. With good organization, training can be accomplished "on-the-job," avoiding a lag between when a person expresses interest in helping and when he or she can actually join in the setup activities. Everyone is happier because "new faces" periodically rotate onto teams. Even seekers can join in when everything is organized. Overall, ascribing order to facility procedures helps tame the turmoil of renting.

Portability

Another critical tactic to counter the aforementioned challenges is to be as portable as possible. This is seen most strikingly in a church's efforts to be lightweight and compact with what they store and transport to and from the facility each week. Although we discovered countless examples of this strategy, here is a sampling to stimulate your thinking:

- Use storage tubs and crates that are durable but made of light plastic. To prevent spills in transit, don't overfill them and discard worn ones.

- Make displays with boards and backdrops that fold flat.

- Whenever possible, use equipment and furnishings available at the meeting place so that you don't have to transport them from somewhere else (e.g., tables, seating, ladders, music stands, TV/VCRs, fans, chalkboards, flags, and overhead projectors).

- Attach sturdy handles and wheels (with casters of proper weight-bearing ratios) to make heavier items feel lighter and move faster.

- If age-appropriate furnishings are needed, bring those that are foldable and made of plastic or aluminum.

- For nurseries, use portable "Pack-n-Play" cribs that fold small and can be carried easily.

- Obtain aluminum and nylon lawn-chair type rocking chairs for the nursery.

- Use tall rolling cabinets that can double for room dividers so that fewer partitions have to be brought on site. Shorter cabinets can be covered and serve as things like refreshment centers and children's registration stations, saving on the number of tables that need to be brought and set up.

- Purchase stacking microphones, because they are lighter and save more space than standard ones.

- Consider using a pulpit made of something like Plexiglas sheets instead of oak.

- Save weight and space with electric drum sets and keyboards.

- Substitute outdoor polyvinyl banners for large wooden or metal signs.

- Make space dividers and backdrops with cloth curtains and PVC frames instead of using heavier portable partitions. If you need to provide an acoustical barrier, affixing thick curtains to telescoping metal posts is usually an adequate alternative to more bulky solutions.

While you strive to make the spiritual experience as substantial as possible, also strive to make the physical experience as lightweight as possible.

Ingenuity helps too, like when the father of a middle schooler recommended the youth game tables be mounted on plastic sawhorses, which cut their combined weight almost in half. Nothing is too small. Shedding a few pounds and a few square feet here and there adds up. Being as portable as possible by using lighter, more compact materials increases facility team efficiency, eases recruiting, retains workers longer, enables more people to help, saves storage space, lessens wear and tear on transportation vehicles, and shortens setup/breakdown. So when you purchase something to be used at the rental site, consider more than the cost—consider its weight!

Support Systems

Facility servants, program leaders, teachers, technicians, and the like should never have to "fend for themselves." If anything, it is *because* they're part of a Nomadic Church that they should be given all the support possible. Every successful Nomadic Church we know of attempts to have a strong, authentic, visionary leadership team that develops, supports, encourages, and resources a growing core of servant-leaders. Churches of any kind rarely flourish without this kind of support.

A critical leadership position at Nomadic Churches is what we've called the "facility coordinator." A few facility coordinators are paid servants; most volunteer. A few are full-time; most are part-time. None are the senior pastor! With input from other leaders, this person is primarily responsible for preventing and responding to the physical and personnel facility-related challenges. This role ensures that at least one mind is focused exclusively on addressing various facility-related challenges.

The facility coordinator usually answers directly to a staff pastor and must be authorized, expected, and empowered to make decisions relevant to this role. Some facility coordinators regularly or periodically participate in the meetings of the main governing body of the church. In the least, a wise nomadic leadership team will seek the coordinator's input when a decision is being considered that may influence or be influenced by facility affairs. Beyond this, assuring that the congregation recognizes this person as an important leader in the church helps alleviate "the most common facility manager complaint." According to the National Association of Church Facility Ministers, their prime grievance "is the lack of credibility commonly afforded the position. Many are given plenty of responsibility but lack the power to make things happen."[4] Nomadic Churches can't afford to make that mistake.

The requirements and responsibilities of this position do not seem to differ drastically among Nomadic Churches. The following are some basic qualities looked for in facility coordinators:

- A growing disciple of Christ with godly character (in some churches this requirement is referred to as "deacon-qualified," based on such passages as Acts 6:1-6 and 1 Tim 3:8-13);

- Well-developed people and time management skills that will translate into the forming and oversight of cohesive, efficient teams;

- A positive mental attitude and an encouraging spirit;

- A self-starter with leadership and/or administrative gifts and abilities; and

- A willingness to work behind the scenes for the advancement of the church.

These and other desired qualities—like being an early riser!—are often ascertained through some sort of interview process by the person the coordinator will report to.

In addition to meeting personal qualifications, the facility coordinator may be responsible to do such things as:

- Interact responsibly with the host agent;

- Plan, schedule, and secure space usage;

- Organize equipment use;

- Submit rental contracts and ensure bills are paid in a timely way;

- Recruit, train, support, and manage facility crews; and

- oversee setup, breakdown, storage, and transportation issues.

In most (unpaid) cases, it's prudent to set a minimum length of a two-year commitment for this position. That's long enough to gain valuable experience but short enough for someone not to feel "indefinitely trapped" in the position. See appendix B for a more detailed sample facility coordinator job description.

The presence of a strong facility coordinator can help prevent every facility-related challenge or lessen its impact.

In addition to facility coordinators, assistant facility coordinators, crew captains, deacons, or people in similar positions are assigned defined responsibilities, such as overseeing one of the task-specific crews identified earlier. Although they don't try to do it all themselves, vocational staff members—including the lead pastor—take an active role in addressing rental challenges. This is clearly a reason that all of the churches we interviewed indicated that strong leadership is integral to preventing and alleviating facility-induced challenges.

Encouragement

Never underestimate the power of encouragement. Affirmation is biblical and it increases volunteers' productivity and longevity. The esteem afforded the facility servant role also makes the position more palatable to potential new recruits. Nobody wants to be stuck in a meaningless role.

We discovered that facility workers who express a higher rate of satisfaction with their ministry also agree most strongly that they feel valued by their church and its leaders.

The churches with facility servants who reported the highest satisfaction also reported lower than average recruitment struggles. Conclusion: Be encouraging!

Here are some ideas that stood out as meaningful encouragement to facility workers we interviewed:

• Regularly acknowledge facility servants in worship services and at special events when they have contributed. This can be done verbally and in printed programs. Creative touches make it more memorable.

• Periodically publicize the facility servants and their contributions in the Sunday worship folder, newsletter, church Web site, or other print media.

• Personally praise workers you bump into as they perform their tasks. A note of appreciation mailed later that week makes an even stronger impact.

• Have every worker who helped set up that morning stand during worship. Then lead the congregation in applause and prayer for them.

• Rather than scurry off to lunch or the next meeting, some lead pastors periodically stay until the doors close and personally thank each servant. Pastor Bruce Johnson of Seneca Creek Community Church put our interview on hold for ninety minutes until he finished thanking each member of the facility crew. When we asked the facilities director if Bruce did this routinely, he answered appreciatively, "That's what he does *every* week."

- Personally participate in some aspect of facility operations when possible, such as at a special event you are not involved in. Like a general in combat, when you spend a few minutes rubbing shoulders in the trenches with your "facility troops" it can invigorate them for weeks.

- Some smaller and midsized churches give the facilities servants more immediate access to pastors and church resources than others might receive. One pastor said, "We treat them like major players." Church leaders should feel more urgency to be available to those sacrificially serving the church.

- As a show of support, some churches go out of their way to make it as easy as possible for the facility coordinator to purchase resources that help the facilities team perform their job faster and better. As an example, the veteran staff coordinator Kris MacFarlane proudly held up his new walkie-talkie, which he and his three crew captains now use to easily communicate from various parts of the facilities during the morning.

- A few churches like New Hope Community Church find it meaningful to lay hands on the facilities servants in a public service and commission them to "take authority over the facilities."

- Organize a campaign to have as many people as possible, if not everybody, assist the regular facility servants on a given week or month. The servants will be encouraged, congregants will better appreciate the role, and you will likely pick up some new helpers in the process!

- Synergy among workers can be heartening. To develop this, many gather for prayer or lighthearted fellowship before or after their setup duties and off site other times of the year. This builds a sense of camaraderie among the facility community.

• Group identity can also be energizing and promote recognition, so many churches prescribe a name for the facility team. An increasingly popular one is "Levites," which is appropriate considering that it refers to the tribe who had responsibility for the *first* portable worship center (see chapter 2).

Consultation

A valuable way to prevent and surmount facility-related challenges is by understanding what other Nomadic Churches have successfully done. Nearly every church we studied mentioned the importance of learning from other homeless churches, especially when in their earlier stages of a plant. This informal underground and a humble "learner's mentality" have spared many mistakes and ineffective responses. That is why we so strongly encourage more and less experienced Nomadic Churches to team together for the greater good of the Body of Christ.

At some point, it may be useful to pay for specialized consulting. Nomadic Churches sometimes employ the services of an interior architect, audiovisual technician, marketing firm, or trade show specialist—each of whom tends to bolster the Sunday experience beyond what one might initially expect. The expense usually saves time and money in the long run. Two helpful organizations that solely target Nomadic Churches are Portable Church Industries and Mobile Church Solutions (Passion for Planting). (See appendixes A and F.)

As more churches are birthed and the experience base broadened, and as the service sector gains more awareness of the portable plight, future Nomadic Churches will undoubtedly have even more assets to draw upon. They will be increasingly distanced from the sentiment expressed by one of our interviewees who was reflecting back to 1989 when his church started: "There was nothing out there—nobody to talk to; no resources."

Responses to Atmospheric Stresses

Propelled by their missional mindset, growing Nomadic Churches refuse to be sidelined until they have the best possible meeting site, even though that means functioning on Sundays in a less-than-ideal environment. As one church leader said, "Renting a school is like renting an apartment; you have to make it your own." We've compiled some key practices to help you overcome the inevitable atmospheric stresses Nomadic Churches face. Other ideas are considered in later chapters in response to different challenges.

Be Prepared and Flexible

Nomadic Churches need to be prepared and flexible because they never know what they may encounter when they arrive on a given Sunday or throughout the morning. The more you prepare for the unexpected, the better off you will be when it happens.

Without having their own supply closets to turn to in case of emergency, contingency plans are a must for Nomadic Churches!

- Keep a back-up location in mind for when the host says you can't use the facilities that weekend. Hotel conference centers, large restaurant rooms, parks, lodges, firehouses, the buildings of Sabbath-observing churches, and other spaces that are unused on Sunday mornings may suffice for at least one weekend (see table 4 in chapter 9 for options). But don't wait until the need arises. A phone call Saturday evening will rarely get you in the next morning. In advance, tell the managers of these locations your needs as a church and ask them what they will require and how much notice you will need to give to use their space. Be prepared to pay a retainer fee and to fill out an unsigned contract to expedite an emergency rental. Also make sure that your facility coordinator and other key leaders (e.g., worship and children's directors) are aware of the alternate site, so that they can develop at least a notional plan for using the facility.

- If the host provides a custodian or other person responsible to interface with you on the weekend, develop a positive relationship with that person. When possible, get a contact number in case he or she fails to show. Also, keep the superintendent's number handy in case you can't reach the custodian.

- Remind your people to dress suitably for unexpected climates. Make a point to offer ample hot drinks on cold days and vice versa if you anticipate an inclement setting.

- If climate control is a perpetual problem, invest in space heaters and cooling fans. These should be strategically placed around the site, like near the main entrance, nurseries, and the worship center.

- A sense of humor never hurts. When one church arrived to find the heat not working, the service began with a mild "aerobic routine" to generate body heat. Later during a "greet one another session," hugs were encouraged. People laughed and the crisis passed with little fanfare. Rarely does it help to ignore a challenge or pretend it doesn't exist.

- Somebody should be on site early enough to combat any unpleasant aromas. A can of disinfectant air freshener should always be part of a supply box and liberally used whenever necessary.

- Never be content to meet in a messy building. An unattractive, unsafe, or unsanitary setting isn't uplifting to members or visitors. Bring your own vacuum, mops, and other light cleaning equipment if none are available for you to use.

- Before congregants arrive, always check the restrooms for an ample supply of soap, toilet paper, and paper towels. If these are not of the same quality you'd use in your own building, bring in the good stuff. Wiping down sinks, picking up trash, and offering disposable hand towels, air freshener, antibacterial soap, sanitary seat covers, and at least a makeshift baby-changing station can make that trip to the bathroom much more pleasant than it would otherwise be.

- In schools, request that the faculty bathrooms be unlocked for the church's use. These are usually much nicer than the student restrooms—and the stall doors are still attached!

- If the facilities appear bleak, liberally place artificial plants and other greenery around the parts of the facility where people congregate. Ask if you can leave them during the week to save on transportation and storage. As more than one church has discovered, the host may even appreciate the extra touch.

- Post banners, posters (mounted on cardboard for repeated use), art, and other decorative touches that are meaningful to the congregation, reflect its identity, and complement the emphasis of the service. Conversely, remove or cover what detracts from that identity or emphasis.

- Place customized church welcome mats in front of the main entrances.

- Bring in portable lights to brighten the auditorium if it is dingy, and make sure the host has a readily accessible stock of spare bulbs for their lights. Some churches have been allowed to mount permanent lights to the ceiling, especially if the host is permitted to use them when needed.

- Keep a supply of spare bulbs (e.g., for projectors) and batteries (e.g., for wireless microphones) in a protected storage bin.

- Hang directional signs throughout the building. Use a type that is noticeable and can easily be moved so that a group's meeting place isn't missed when they have to change from their usual room.

- Strategically locate information displays, resource carts, and guest reception tables in main lobbies and high traffic areas, provided doing so will not make those areas impassable.

- Provide a refreshment center. We've seen them range from hot drinks and light pastries to full-service food stands with veggie trays, cotton candy, snow cones, portable cappuccino machines, and more. Coffee pots with "instant on" features save time. The smell of things like fresh coffee, bread, and popcorn can also subconsciously enliven the atmosphere.

Provide a Positive Parking Experience

When a parking lot is so full that people have to drive around and around, the tendency is to give up, go home, and not return. Some Christians might even rationalize the problem by saying, "I'll stay home and leave room for those who need it." If there is sufficient space but other parking problems exist, attendees may enter the building with a hint of exasperation. Here are some ways successful Nomadic Churches have sought to minimize the parking issues we previously mentioned.

No matter how great the things happening within a facility are, a poor parking situation will mean less people get in to experience them.

- When looking for a meeting place, make sure there are more than enough parking spaces for your congregation's present needs and to have plenty of room to grow. A good rule of thumb for parking is one space for every two people on the campus.

- Put signs in the parking lot to welcome people to the church. Banners and "sandwich boards" are best because of their portability.

- Consider implementing a "parking lot ministry." This team greets each vehicle with a friendly smile, directs traffic, and can point people toward available parking spaces and the main entrance. It is not unusual for this team to use walkie-talkies to coordinate their efforts.

- Designate several choice parking spaces for "first time guests." Signs indicating this can be affixed to a durable pole with a weighted base, to a pointed stake that can be driven into the ground, or to existing signs like those reserved for school faculty.

- Although it may be tempting to park a transport vehicle right by the entrance, remember to reserve handicapped parking spaces for their intended use. After unloading equipment, move transport vehicles to the farthest point of the property. If you are short on parking, move them off of the premises.

- Ask core members to park in the spaces farthest from the facility to allow guests to have the choicest spots. This courtesy will catch on more readily if it's modeled by the leadership.

- In order not to irritate neighbors or jeopardize your contract, check with the rental host before parking outside the specified parameters—especially on a school's athletic fields.

- Seek the advice of local authorities before parking along streets. As involved as it may be, providing shuttles from an approved parking area may ultimately be less disruptive than finding a new rental site altogether, especially for large churches or those in communities with no other rental options.

- If safety is a concern, police have been known to provide traffic control for churches. If they won't and you sense the need for traffic direction beyond that of church servants, consider hiring off-duty police.

- If you are in an area where snow or ice is an issue, find out who the host contracts to clear their lots. Be sure they know your Sunday schedule *before* a storm hits.

- Bring or borrow salt, sand, and shovels in case some parking spaces or sidewalks are not cleared to your satisfaction.

- Ask the host to inform you *in advance* of any on-site activities, like a sports tournament or seminar, that will result in the parking lot being filled to capacity when you need it. By doing so, you can plan alternatives, like encouraging carpooling, hiring shuttle busses, adjusting your meeting time, or moving the morning service to another location for the day.

- If there isn't a drop-off lane, consider using traffic cones to make one near the main entrance, especially if some parking areas are far away.

Granted, parking isn't part of the Great Commission. But a lack of parking sure can hinder your efforts to carry it out! A consistently full or faulty parking lot is enough reason by itself to consider finding a new meeting site, adding a second worship service at the rented site, investigating multiple-campus options, or even planting a new fellowship altogether.

Give Priority Space to Worship and Children

Worship and children are two areas you can not shortchange when it comes to addressing environmental strains. To fail here is to fail all around. The goal is to ensure that the space is optimized for your activities and reflects your values more than those of the host. As lead pastor Bob Hyatt of The Evergreen Community (www.evergreenlife.org) in Portland, Oregon, comments, "We believe that everything preaches—including our space. So we try to make sure the space is saying something our community actually wants it to say."

The key to the worship space is to ensure that it is conducive to the type of worship you desire. Often this means blocking out distracting or inappropriate objects. Arranging chairs in an optimal configuration can help accomplish this.[5] No matter how hectic the morning has been, the front area should be neat and attractive, since people focus their attention on it for so long each Sunday. Even something as small as using dark power extension cords instead of the distracting standard yellow or orange ones can make a difference.

Many churches use curtains, partitions, or other dividers to form a backdrop along the wall(s) people face and around the sides of the worship space, so that all they see are the projection screens, the people leading worship, and any decorative objects placed on or in front of the backdrops. This can enhance acoustics and make an overwhelmingly large room feel smaller and more intimate. Churches that meet in auditoriums that are at least 40 percent empty each Sunday can take the lead from other churches and erect dividers to keep the critical mass and its energy in the area closer to the stage. In the absence of dividers, a similar effect can be achieved by setting up less chairs or roping off the back rows in places with fixed seating. When your church nears 80 percent capacity of your present space, it's time to prepare to add a service or look for a new site.

A clean, quiet nursery that is close to the worship space allows visitors to feel more comfortable leaving their child in a new place. The continuity of at least one nursery attendant serving nearly every week is important enough to pay someone for, if necessary. This person should always be an adult. Youth are acceptable help only if they are supervised by an adult. Be sure to have a quality brochure and laminated signs that explain how you care for the babies and their toys and cribs. As you are able, provide each parent with a pager or some other "quick alert" system in case they are needed during the service.

Some other critical safety measures for the nursery include finding or making a space with padded or covered floors; not putting walking babies where they can poke their fingers in the eyes of or otherwise injure the crib babies; not having anything sharp or hot in the room such as scissors, coffee, or a space heater; discarding small toys that present a choking hazard; having sanitary wipes, disposable gloves, and disinfectant for diaper changes; and covering all electrical outlets.

One of the more difficult nursery needs is some kind of "cry room" for nursing mothers. With some ingenuity most churches can find or make (usually with dividers like curtains or tall rolling cabinets) a suitable private spot. Ideally, it will be close to the worship area but far enough away for noise not to be a distraction. Moms are usually provided secondary participation in the service through video cameras, monitors, or speakers set up in a hall or room adjacent to the "sanctuary." If you're in doubt over what would be best to do in your situation, just ask a couple new mothers for suggestions!

The children's areas often require special attention, especially in movie theaters or in schools where the rooms are decorated with material that may be inappropriate for little eyes. Do a "visual sweep" of each room *before* children arrive. Although children don't bring their parents to church, parents are far more likely to return if their children have an appropriately memorable experience.

"One of the biggest questions we face with children's ministry is security. We pick only those areas where there is one way in or out for our children, so that people don't have a reason to go down to that area except for the kids—not even the rest rooms. And if you're not wearing a badge, you are stopped. We have a person who roams the halls like a security system. We want positive control of every child. . . . The parent has to have the same badge number as the child even if we know them."
—Todd Wilson, Executive Pastor, New Life Christian Church

To counter privacy concerns, many churches reserve an area in the facility that is as private and soundproof as possible. They use it for all sorts of unexpected occasions, such as parents who need to speak privately with or discipline their children, crisis counseling, evangelistic follow-up, counting the morning offering, or emergency leadership meetings. Even smaller schools usually have a suitable place, such as teachers' lounges, isolated rooms and offices, and areas behind the stage. Scout these places out in advance so you can use them and point others toward them as need arises.

Storage Space Takes Creativity

Storage shortages can stress even strong Nomadic Churches. But to endure, the strain must be neutralized. Here are several ways effective churches dilute their storage dilemmas:

- Storage needs typically increase as a church grows, so don't wait to secure more space until you need it. Nomadic Churches always need it!

- When choosing a rental site, prioritize any that offer ample storage. It is not the only criterion for a suitable meeting place, but even a modest storage area can edge out a facility that offers none. That's why on-site storage is always one of the top site selection considerations of the churches we studied.

- Make sure any guaranteed on-site storage space is specified in the rental contract. If it is retracted there will be a better chance of getting a comparable area or of being compensated for the loss in some other way.

- If you rent a place with little or no on-site storage, periodically and politely make your storage needs known to the host. At least you'll be "in line" if something opens up, as it periodically does in places like warehouses and public schools.

- If you must go off site for storage, one large place is better than several smaller storage areas, because it makes transporting church belongings to and from the facility quicker and easier.

- If prices are comparable, renting the storage garage that is nearest to where the church meets will save time.

- Consider sharing the cost of a large storage space with another Nomadic Church in town, or at least ask how they meet their storage needs to get ideas.

- Look for suitable office and storage space combinations. South Potomac Church (www.southpotomac.org) in White Plains, Maryland, enjoyed a two-story office suite that sat over a built-in storage garage in an industrial park. Their senior pastor, Brent Brooks, noted that having everything in the same location was a plus for transportation, equipment maintenance, supply restocking, and loading and unloading. The fact that it was just minutes from the meeting site was a bonus.

73

- Canvass members and encourage them to explore their networks to find adequate, economical storage space. Make VIPs out of people who have and are willing to use their empty garages, business warehouse space, trailers, or large vehicles to help with storage and transportation.

- Because of the risk of theft and vandalism, avoid storing expensive equipment in trailers that will be left in unsecured areas during the week. If they must be, several churches we interviewed told us that armored reinforcements are mandatory!

- Remember to be as lightweight and compact as possible when it comes to church supplies and equipment (see above). The amount saved on storage space can add up significantly over the years.

- Creativity helps, too. One church told us how they built two durable locking sheds within a secured area of the school where they meet. How'd they get this special dispensation? One of the two sheds was for the school to have and use!

Responses to Host-Tenant Strains

We cannot overstress the importance of a church's relationship with its rental host. The better the relationship, the fewer potential surprises and disasters the church will experience and the greater positive influence it will exert on host personnel. Take note: Churches who report the best relationships with their hosts also have the most pleasant and longest tenures at their rental sites!

The better the relationship with the host, the fewer surprises and disasters a Nomadic Church experiences.[6]

One of the best examples we've seen of developing a good host-tenant relationship is New Hope in Honolulu. Over the few years they have been using the high school, they have poured hundreds of thousands of dollars into the school with no strings attached. Just recently the church installed air conditioning in the main auditorium. We think it is fair to say that New Hope has a home as long as they need it. If you can make your church an irresistibly positive benefit to your host, you will have a happy home too!

Developing a solid relationship with the custodial staff is one of the smartest and most strategic things a Nomadic Church could ever do.

Not all churches can afford such costly expenditures. So what can Nomadic Churches do to foster a better relationship? Here are some suggestions:

- Never surprise the host. Always keep them informed of your plans in advance and preferably in writing. Your church isn't the only thing on their mind, so follow up with courteous reminders as appropriate.

- Have one or two main people, like a facility coordinator, visit with the host on a regular basis at a time convenient to them. Discuss relevant facility matters. For every request you make, aim to make an offer to be a better tenant or otherwise help the host. A pastor from New Life Christian Church in Virginia visits the school they rent nearly every week, and they have enjoyed several years in a spacious high school with strong regional draw.

- As any experienced landlord will tell you, good tenants are worth their weight in gold. They're also slower to be ousted. Be an exceptional tenant who goes above and beyond the requirements of the rental contract. Aim to leave the building in the same condition, if not better, than when you arrived. When you see something broken, fix it if it is within your budget. When you see a dirty area, clean it up. If an area needs painting, offer to paint it. In other words, "Do to others as you would have them do to you" (Luke 6:31).

- To reduce the chance of being unfairly blamed for damages, establish and enforce a policy that all church workers promptly report anything they break or use up—including the chalk. We hear that it's often the "little things" that most annoy the host. Also, immediately report to the on-site custodian anything you discover to be broken or missing when you arrive. Even when these measures fail, some leaders admit they have paid for things they were confident they didn't break. As one pastor told us, "Replacing a dead hermit crab we didn't kill is a lot cheaper than finding a new place to meet!"

- When renting school rooms, it is good to periodically draw maps or take digital pictures of all the rooms, so that everything is rearranged the way it was before you arrived. For one church we interviewed, this simple "leave no trace" measure eliminated roughly 85 percent of teacher complaints.

- When renting in schools, graciously switch rooms when a teacher perpetually indicates displeasure at the church's use of her or his room.

- Remember that your presence is not automatically a "win-win situation" for the host—and then work to make it one! One church bought a supply of snow shovels that the school could use in exchange for the school storing them on site. Another had new stage flooring and curtains added to the auditorium. Still another donated their portable dramatic and musical equipment for the school's off-site winter program. The examples are endless because all growing Nomadic Churches have learned how critical this principle is.

- Figure out the "functional hierarchy" of the host personnel in the organization you rent from. There are usually three key players you need to work with at a school: The Sunday custodian, the superintendent, and the principal, usually in this order. We've often heard that the head custodian of the school usually calls the shots. In some cases the teachers can request that their rooms not be used by the church, but the custodian has the final say and the principal seems to do whatever he says as well. Knowing who the main player is when making a decision will help you tailor your efforts to get the results you need.

- Consider giving an annual Christmas gift to the school. Some churches give a gift to every teacher whose classroom is used by the church; others periodically leave notes, baked goods, and teaching supplies for the teachers. Imagine the result when teachers actually *want* the church to use their room for classes!

- Most churches give a little extra to the custodial staff employed to care for their site. This is important enough to be included on the job description of some facility coordinators. Holidays, birthdays, and three-day weekends are a popular time to give a "financial bonus," flowers, tickets to a sporting event, or a wide variety of thoughtful gifts. As with all gift giving, the better you know the person, the better you can tailor the gift.

- When renting from schools or community centers, some churches offer their bands to the host to play secular music during special holidays. Bay Area Community Church told us that their worship team's appearance at a school event was just enough to convince the principal to renew their contract for an extra year—even though they had technically outstayed the time they were allowed to rent the school!

- Although it shouldn't be the first reaction to a compromised rental contract, don't hesitate to seek legal advice when a situation warrants. Thanks to the *Lamb's Chapel* and *Good News* cases, the law is (at least for now) still on the side of extending the same public facility rental rights and rates to churches as are offered to other outside groups. See appendix A for some places to learn about legal issues that affect Nomadic Churches.

- Turn adversity into advancement whenever possible. When Willamette Christian Church in West Linn, Oregon (www.willamettechurch.com), outgrew their building, they began meeting for two Sunday services in a local middle school. This worked out well for them, until the school district hired a new superintendent—one who apparently didn't like the idea of churches meeting in schools. He banned school building use on all holiday weekends. Imagine the impact on a church! Rather than cancel services, however, Pastor Gary Snavely turned this setback into a success. For the first holiday, Independence Day, the church sponsored an event in a local park. They were able to hold a worship service and draw unchurched people from the community to the festivities they had planned.

- Be sure to have adequate liability insurance that specifically covers your congregation, its transportation vehicles, and the rental site.

- Pray for the host personnel and your relationship with them in public services and private leadership meetings. It will open otherwise locked doors and sensitize listeners to the spiritual dimension of the host-tenant relationship. Also, tactfully invite the host personnel to worship with you and to share their prayer requests with you. Some are surprisingly enthusiastic about doing so, and it has led to some amazing stories of spiritual awakening.

Although it may never be reciprocated, Nomadic Churches have a responsibility and opportunity to show Christian charity to the host.

Remember, you are *God's* church and how you relate to others says a lot about who you really are!

Sometimes intuitively and usually imperfectly, great churches live out their biblical mandate to "be wise in the way you act toward outsiders; make the most of every opportunity" (Col 4:5) and "if it is possible, as far as it depends on you, live at peace with everyone" (Rom 12:18; cf. Phil 1:27; 1 Tim 3:7; Titus 3:1-2; Heb 13:18; 1 Pet 2:11-17). Because of their Christian attitude with the host, Pastor Kyle Austin of Occoquan Bible Church was asked to conduct a memorial service in the school auditorium for an unchurched student who died. Later, this opened the door for church members to be invited to mentor students, start a community basketball league with the local ministerial association, and volunteer to be hall monitors during school hours! In your zeal to reach the community, remember that host personnel *are* the community.

Talk Time for Teams

For Pre-Plant Teams

- In addition to what we've offered, what else might you do to prevent or lessen the impact of the facility-related challenges raised in the previous chapter?

- What teams do you need to have in place to be prepared for meeting in a rental facility? How will you recruit and encourage these servants?

- Draw up a master list of what you need to bring to your meeting site each week. How can you make these items more compact and lightweight? How will you transport them? Where will you store them?

- What requirements will you establish for a facility coordinator, and who will at least initially fulfill that role? Write a sample ministry (job) description.

- Are there any Nomadic Churches from whom you can glean ways to deal with physical and personnel challenges? Draw up a list and plan to visit and dialogue with as many as possible within driving distance before your launch date.

- After a walk-through of your new meeting site, use the information above to organize an action plan for setup, site manipulation, and breakdown before your first corporate gathering.

A comprehensive "run-through" is strongly encouraged at least a week in advance.

- Do you have the right kind and amount of insurance coverage for the rental site?

- What have you learned about being prepared, flexible, and intentional in responding to facility-related challenges?

- In reference to things like parking and storage, what does this chapter imply about the kind of meeting facility you should seek to rent?

- Does your anticipated approach to ministry need to be adjusted in order to carry out the responses offered above? How?

For Post-Plant Teams

- In addition to what we've offered, what else have you done to prevent or lessen the impact of physical and personnel challenges like those raised in the previous chapter?

- Evaluate your Sunday teams. How can you strengthen them? Do you need to add any or divide any into more task-specific crews? How can you alleviate the stress of recruiting servants for these teams?

- How can you make your church facility operations more lightweight? More organized?

- If you haven't yet, consider establishing a facility coordinator position. If you have one, how can you better use and empower this person?

- On a scale of 1 to 10 (10 being the highest), how well do you encourage your facility servants? What ideas, either suggested above or your own, will you implement to increase your score? Why not ask some of your own volunteers for tangible ideas? Take some time to pray for your laborers.

- Is there a new church in your area with whom you could share your experience in handling physical and personnel challenges? Why not initiate the contact? You'll likely benefit from the relationship too.

- What steps can you take to strengthen your relationship with your rental host and its personnel? As you make concrete plans, take time to pray for your host.

- Which of the suggestions above or others you have thought of will you implement to help prevent or alleviate your facility-related physical and personnel challenges? Who will be responsible to do so? What is the timeline for beginning and evaluating these new measures?

CHAPTER SIX

REVEALING PROGRAM AND SPECIAL EVENT CHALLENGES

As important as the Sunday worship service is in the life of a local church, it is never the sole focus of a growing church. Outsiders might think that a homeless congregation can't extend themselves much beyond Sunday services, because of the energy that's required just to "do church" on a given weekend. However, many life-changing programs and special events fill the calendars of vibrant Nomadic Churches. This chapter examines facility-related challenges they face in the process of planning and performing these ministries.

"We've allowed the marketplace to be the place where ministry is done. We're trying to be an Acts church. It's not easy. But I have a saying: 'I have to get the Church out of the church, in order to be the Church!' "—Wayne Cordeiro, Pastor of New Hope Community Church

Program Challenges

Our research reveals a long list of facility-related programmatic challenges. Like before, we have grouped them into three subcategories to make the discussion more focused and manageable: (1) space constraints, (2) equipment complexities, and (3) security concerns.

Program challenges refer to any mild to acute problem, limitation, or stress faced by an ongoing program of a Nomadic Church due partly or largely to the fact that it rents temporary facilities.

Space Constraints

Although many Nomadic Churches have robust programs, some leaders admit to postponing certain ministries because they do not have the facilities to do everything they desire. Pastor Martin Occurto of Trinity Community Church speaks for at least some Nomadic Churches when he says, "We're maxed out on our worship and classroom space."

Some examples of programs that have been put on hold due to space shortages are certain training and Christian education programs; midweek "New Community" services; community-targeted enrichment classes and sports leagues; compassionate ministries like meals for the needy, clothing distribution, and reading programs; and midweek children's and youth ministries. The absence of sufficient space can prevent having a special area for things like prayer, counseling, nursing mothers, a church resource room (library), and a "VIP Room" for welcoming and interacting with newcomers.

On Sundays, children's ministry directors are constrained to keep learning centers far more simple than they'd like. Certain groups that would otherwise be split are kept together. A combined junior high and high school group is a frequent casualty of the space crunch. Conversely, many rental sites do not have enough large areas to hold all the large group meetings on a Sunday. It gets even more complicated when a church's preferred program involves both large and small group meetings (e.g., Willow Creek's "Promiseland" children's ministry approach).

A wider variety of adult classes on Sundays are forfeited when space limits the number that can be offered simultaneously.

Teachers must contend with the noise of other classes when several hallways are used for class space or when groups have to meet in the corners of gymnasiums. Still, competing with other voices is easier than competing with the kids' temptation to play with equipment in gyms, game tables in community centers, and pet cages in schools.

The inability to customize or manipulate the space designated for a program comes up often when talking to leaders of various ministry areas. Nursery directors long for more and better equipment. "You can only bring in so many Pack-n-Play cribs," said one nursery supervisor. A preschool director mused, "I only want *one thing* in our new church building: a bathroom built for little kids." Even if a church owns office space that alleviates some space constraints, it still must be shared with multiple groups. Youth leaders await the day they have a specially designated room to customize as they see fit. Those ragged old couches sure beat the seating of most rental sites!

Like all Sunday programs, whatever functional or aesthetic changes leaders make to their rented rooms, halls, or areas must be taken down, packed up, stored, transported, and picked up the next Sunday to begin the process all over again. And, lest the wrath of a host be invoked, the room must be put back exactly the way it was found. Try doing that with a dozen sixth-grade boys in a cramped room!

Many of the physical challenges cited in chapter 4 have programmatic consequences. If parking and storage are tough on the church, they're at *least* as tough on programs. If poor weather, construction, utility breakdown, or cleaning shuts down all or part of the facility, programs suffer right along with the rest of the church. If the doors are opened late (either the main entrance *or* individual meeting rooms), programs lose valuable time or must make alternate arrangements—often at the last minute. When foul odors, dirty facilities, a poor climate, privacy issues, and tension with the host affect the church, they also affect its programs. If there are distractions in the "sanctuary," there are probably even more disturbing "distractions" in the classrooms.

Facility-related staffing challenges also exist. The fact that it takes so many people such a long time to set up and break down can keep some servants from participating in or leading other

Sunday programs. Other people are more reluctant or unable (e.g., because of a small apartment or vehicle) to serve in a ministry that requires their involvement in storing, transporting, and setting up for the program. Directors of children's ministries must sometimes staff an additional person beyond their preferred teacher-student ratio, just so there are enough workers still with the children when another worker needs to take a child for a long distance walk to the only age-appropriate bathroom in the facility. And, of course, if a church has to relocate again, its programs will be on hold until the place is secured. Then they'll once again have to be recontextualized to the new facility.

Equipment Complexities

Most programs need some type of equipment to function optimally. Although less expansive than the previous subcategory, Nomadic Churches face certain complexities involving equipment and supplies. Nursery cribs, craft supplies, teaching materials, age-appropriate furnishings, children's toys, TV/VCRs, projection equipment, white boards, CD players, carpets, curtains, and many other items need to be stored, transported, set up, repacked or taken down, and driven somewhere to be restored—all within a few hours time. If those same things are needed for a midweek meeting, it has to be done all over again. That's part of why heavier, bulkier, and elective program materials are sometimes reluctantly forfeited, regardless of how advantageous they may be to a program.

Not having onsite storage rooms or at least a closet is a frustration for ministry leaders and helpers. It is even more disheartening to have been given some storage space only to have it taken away when the host needs it back. The constant shuffling of equipment also hastens its deterioration. Since there is already hardly enough room to transport what programs need, it is more difficult to stock spare parts or replacement supplies for when something breaks or runs out Sunday morning. Nomadic Churches near a Wal-Mart (for emergency purchases) and FedEx Kinko's (for emergency copies) are truly blessed.

School buildings present their own set of issues. The "one size" onsite equipment and furnishings are not suited to every age-graded program. The school's equipment that may be available to the tenant must sometimes be rented. It may also be locked away or malfunctioning the morning it is needed, causing further disruptions to program plans. The bell system has been known to ring on its weekly schedule throughout a Sunday morning. Of course, there's the occasional false fire alarm, and when one goes off at a school the fire department is obligated by law to respond.

One of the most equipment-intensive programs of the church is the worship ministry. Transportation vehicles are often filled with instruments and audiovisual equipment, and these same items tend to dominate the storage space. Most effective Nomadic Churches have multiple-person contemporary worship bands that are supported by a hoard of equipment. This equipment has to be retrieved and set up not just once each week, but multiple times when you consider band practice, midweek worship services, and any other program or event during the week that requires worship equipment. Having multiple music teams—worship bands, children's groups, adult choirs—may mean crews wrestle with this equipment nearly every day in a given week.

A critical component of the whole worship ministry operation is audiovisual support. Churches frequently have to improvise a "sound room," often by laying a portable soundboard across the backs of chairs, which in tight quarters takes up valuable seating. Technical training, like that needed to operate a sophisticated sound system, requires focused effort. It doesn't help that Nomadic Churches must frequently assimilate new persons into this important support ministry.

Whereas a typical church could train a new technician any time throughout the week, Nomadic Churches have a limited instruction period.

Since media setup usually takes longer than any other single aspect of the setup process, there is little time for training after the sound system is set up on Sunday. Thus, there are times that the "sanctuary" must be rented for special training sessions because instruction is best done in the target environment. Otherwise, the whole system must be set up elsewhere—once again.

Security Concerns

Security-related concerns also surfaced in our research as a valid facility-related challenge, although not as intense or common as some others. In some ways, it is a greater challenge for Nomadic Churches to be safe and secure than for those with permanent buildings.

In today's world, a church simply can't afford to neglect security, and Nomadic Churches must double the efforts to keep their people and property safe.

Meeting facilities represent unique security challenges for a rental organization. Unlike most church buildings, it is not uncommon to see people not associated with the church walking through the building in a rented facility. In larger churches where congregants don't know everyone, identifying these "strangers" can be especially difficult. The issue is made more complex because of the desire to be welcoming to visitors, not overly wary of them.

Many places have multiple entrances on all sides of its building. Because janitors often work on Sundays when the church is meeting, some of these doors remain unlocked and allow easy entry to potential offenders. Because churches rarely use all the space at their rental site, there are also many "hiding" places. Other times, an outside group will rent a portion of the building or a school's activity fields for an event. This can also inject confusion as to who legitimately belongs with children and who does not. Moreover, since some places like schools are perceived as "public property," people from the community—especially children who attend the school during the week—sometimes feel as if they can "roam the halls" during services.

These issues can make attendees feel uncomfortable. Other times, church equipment has been damaged or stolen. The lack of an established nursery at most sites introduces its own set of security and safety issues, as do the bathrooms without locking stall doors. The absence of posted emergency evacuation plans, first-aid kits, and fire extinguishers in some rental sites also raises safety concerns. Because they regularly face conditions that they would not tolerate in their own building, Nomadic Churches have to remain vigilant.

Special Event Challenges

From casual coffee houses to educational seminars, special events are a critical component of modern church life. Since every growing Nomadic Church offers many meaningful special events throughout the year, the question isn't *if* any can be done. The issue is what facility-related obstacles prevent special events from being done as easily, quickly, efficiently, or inexpensively as they might otherwise be done if the church possessed its own facilities. Unlike programs, these events are not generally planned to happen regularly or frequently, nor are they generally audience-specific (e.g., it is not a weekly women's Bible study or a normally scheduled youth group meeting). But they are just as important to the ministry of a thriving congregation.

Special event challenges refer to any mild to severe facility-induced limitation, inconvenience, or struggle faced by a Nomadic Church when conducting or trying to conduct a church event.

Most of the issues that affect ministry programs also affect special events. For example, if storage, setup, breakdown, transportation, space, furnishings, cleanliness, lighting, atmosphere, parking, climate, safety, recruiting, and security are obstacles for programs, they are at *least* as much of an intense concern for special events—and sometimes more. If the parking lot is almost 80 percent full during a regular weekend service, consider what might happen during a special event. To see other examples for yourself, just re-read chapter 4 and the first half of this chapter with special events in mind.

Because many of the issues that could fairly be raised here have already been mentioned, the remainder of this chapter is divided into just two comparatively brief sections: (1) event impediments and (2) event inconveniences.

Event Impediments

Some of the churches we studied said that they have postponed certain events until they secure a permanent building. Even the "simplest" event requires extra time, energy, people, and money. Therefore, some large-scale events are the quickest to be cut from the annual objectives. Musical concerts, dramas, conferences, community fairs, regional equipping seminars, sports camps, and other large events are among those most frequently deferred or downsized. More than one church has been told that "outside bands" are not permitted on the rental premises, dashing their hopes of sponsoring a concert. After naming a couple of ministries they had decided not to attempt, one pastor admitted, "There are probably more. After a while you automatically filter out the things you know you can't do."

Less grandiose events are also impeded by the portable context. One church's pastoral staff told us they have performed numerous weddings in their seven-year history—but never at the same place twice. Baptisms typically require alternative, off-site arrangements. Because of this, they are sometimes held less frequently than leaders would like. Memorial services; special worship and prayer gatherings; and Christmas Eve, Good Friday, and Thanksgiving services are also rarely held at the regular meeting site, forcing either abandonment or creative alternatives.

Outreach and after-church events involving meals are also bypassed more frequently than some churches would like, due to the lack of kitchen facilities at the rental site. Similarly, picnics, potlucks, sports tournaments, summer children's programs (like Vacation Bible School), and spontaneous prayer events in response to a regional or national tragedy can't be held on church grounds. Even if a rental site is suited for some of these events, it may not be *available* when desired.

Event Inconveniences

In the process of carrying out special events, Nomadic Churches face numerous inconveniences, some of which are implied in the preceding pages. Leaders suggested several other examples, a chief one being that *additional space requires additional money.* The longer and more times a place is used, the more it costs. Even public parks require payment from groups. Churches spend extra time and money for event rehearsals and for the additional wear and tear caused by increased setup and breakdown.

Some places require a "Special Use Permit" be purchased and approved up to a year in advance. This forces churches to plan events inordinately early. A change in facility management or school administration can change the rules for special events even after they are planned. The rental site itself might change for the worse from the time it's contracted to the time of the actual event, like when Bay Area Community Church went to practice a dramatic production only to find several burned out lights and half the stage under repair.

Even decorating for holiday events can be a hassle. Christmas decorations aren't nearly as spiffy as they might be. After all, "It's stressful enough for a family to set up one Christmas tree," a pastor noted, "much less do it quickly four or more times in a month" for services and events. But Nomadic Churches do just that. In fact, they do a lot to dismiss or decrease the many program and event challenges that confront them. The next chapter will explore how they do so.

Talk Time for Teams

For Pre-Plant Teams

- What facility-related challenges have surfaced in this chapter that you may not have considered before? Can you think of other obstacles that might threaten to derail your ministries?

- Discuss what you think should be your "priority programs" (i.e., mission-critical ministries you'll begin as soon as or soon after your public launch). What facility-related challenges might you face as you initiate or develop these?

- What special events are you committed to hold in your first year as a church, irrespective of where you meet? Why? How?

• How does the information in this chapter affect what kind of rental facility you seek to secure for church services, programs, and events?

• Does this chapter alter your attitude or values toward programs and events? Modify how you might approach them?

For Post-Plant Teams

• Can you identify with the facility-related challenges described in this chapter? If so, which ones? If not, why? Share your stories and perspectives with each other.

• What other examples of facility-related program and event challenges could you add to those presented above?

• How, if at all, have these challenges altered your commitment to or perspective on programs and events during your tenure as a Nomadic Church?

• How does this chapter and your discussion affect your thinking, feelings, attitudes, values, and actions toward:
    programs,
    special events,
    your meeting site,
    your equipment,
    your ministry volunteers, and
    your future plans?

CHAPTER SEVEN

RESPONDING TO PROGRAM AND SPECIAL EVENT CHALLENGES

It's Thursday night. A pair of giggly greeters meet you at the door and hand you a ticket for the prize giveaway. Your son is given a towel, which he is told he'll "need" for the game later on. They offer to take your picture to post on the bulletin board along with pictures of dozens of other teenagers and their leaders. Already the smell of popcorn and decaf espresso fills your nostrils.

"Never do more programs than you can do well."—Jeff Carroll, Trinity Community Church

As you walk in, you see kids catching up on the week while they lie on tattered beanbags strewn haphazardly about the room. Unpaid servant leaders—you can tell them by the logo on their T-shirts—mingle with the teens. One lady is praying in a corner with a girl who looks upset. In another corner three teens work playfully at the art expression table. A tall information display tells the story of the upcoming mission trip to Mexico. Beside it sits a literature rack crammed full of flyers, forms, sign-ups, and calendars. You hear laughter, several guys fooling around with the drums, and beeping video games whose volume is loud enough to drown out the music being piped in.

Your son grins good-bye and heads over to play air hockey with the guys from his small group. You shake your head as you turn to leave. For a moment, you forgot that you were dropping him off in the cafeteria of your local elementary school.

This is not a dream. Similar scenes are enacted in the most unlikely places across the country. For sure, the smorgasbord of programs and events that Nomadic Churches offer requires proactive planning and intentional responding. But rather than recoil at this prospect, the flourishing churches we've studied embrace it. In the process, they provide their congregation and community with a wide assortment of sound and successful ministries.

Still, as we discovered in chapter 6, the challenges are real. And they must be realistically addressed. That is our goal in this chapter. In a way, almost all of the responses to physical and personnel challenges in chapter 5 could be repeated here (see figure 3), so you may wish to review them or at least to keep them in mind as you read this chapter.

Space constraints never stop effective nomadic leaders from customizing the space they do have on Sunday mornings to fit their programs or creating dynamic programs that fit their space.

Responses to Program Challenges

If you plan on remaining in rented facilities for years like most Nomadic Churches, you must find a way around every challenge to any ministry that is critical to your mission. When considering facility-related program challenges, the key issue lies in the answer to this question: Are we renting short- or long-term? If short-term, you can live with some of the constraints for a while without them crippling your mission.

A gritty determination propels healthy Nomadic Churches to creatively solve the challenges posed by renting space. That ability, whether intuitive or learned, is one of the most significant ways an effective Nomadic Church is distinguished from an ineffective one. To show some of the fruit of this problem-solving, we offer suggestions that align with the same three subcategories that guided the discussion in chapter 6: (1) space constraints, (2) equipment complexities, and (3) security concerns.

The way leaders overcome facility issues to provide thriving ministries is one of the chief things that separates the effective Nomadic Church from the ineffective.

Combat Space Constraints

The successful Nomadic Churches we studied have a diverse programmatic menu that is sustained by resourcefulness, resolve, creativity, and flexibility. Here are some ways space constraints are tamed and terrific programs unleashed:

- Rent additional space at your usual meeting place for your priority programs before or during your corporate worship service(s). Some churches even rent their same meeting site on Sunday afternoon or evening for ministries.

- Be willing to rent additional off-site space for crucial ministries instead of putting them on hold. Because a program needs less room than the whole church, you can usually rent space somewhere in the community at a fraction of what it costs to rent space for the whole church on Sunday. For example, your whole congregation may not fit in the meeting room of the local fire station, but perhaps your recovery ministry can—and, as New Life found out, sometimes for free! Others, like Crossroads Community (www.crossrdschurch.org) in Dyer, Indiana, rent separate space in the community that their youth ministry has renovated and personalized to their group.

- Having an office at the rental site would be a very rare luxury. But smaller rooms, teachers' lounges, the end of empty halls, space behind stage curtains, and other unused areas in the facility can be outfitted for smaller programs and meetings that might otherwise be held in a pastor's study or other office on a Sunday morning.

- Every church we studied makes culturally relative enhancements. Take the advice of a youth pastor who had just helped cover the entire ceiling of their large lecture hall with a real parachute: "We can't let meeting in a school stop us from reaching these kids." An old saying finds new life in the Nomadic Church: "Bloom where you're planted!"

- Use curtains, partitions, rolling cabinets, or other dividers to transform a large room into more learning centers or meeting places for smaller groups. However, so that there are fewer distractions and less competing noise, don't assign too many groups to the same large area.

- When you can't adjust the facility, adjust your format. There's no rule about how many groups should meet on a Sunday morning. If your rental site has few large group areas, offer more and smaller classes. If there are few intimate spaces, combine smaller groups into larger ones. If this doesn't work, move them off site to a time later in the week. It's easier to change your approach to a ministry than to change the building it meets in.

- Diminish the distractions. Put away sports equipment, cover up game tables, and otherwise mitigate the tempting distractions caused when children's programs are held in gyms, recreation rooms, and the like. Otherwise, move adult groups into those areas.

- Prioritize programs for the littlest ones. Great Nomadic Churches do whatever is necessary to make a great nursery. They bring padded carpets, plastic toy and book containers, portable cribs with mobiles, sign-in stations, gates and containment fences, rocking chairs, curtains, changing tables, bins for personal belongings, radios, laminated instructional signs, and more. Accordingly, most leaders we interviewed report that attendees are generally confident in their church's nursery accommodations. As hard as it may be, listening empathetically to the "complaints" of parents who are dissatisfied can lead to an even stronger children's ministry.

- Assign groups of the youngest children to classrooms that are closest to restrooms. This is more convenient for teachers, is less distracting to others meeting in the facility at the same time, and results in less time that workers need to leave their students to take a child for a bathroom break down the hall.

- A resource center ("church library") doesn't have to be a luxury only available to churches with buildings. This is important enough to the discipleship-driven philosophy of one church we studied that each Sunday they roll out several enclosed carts from their trailer so that members can conveniently check out resources in the lobby of the school where they meet. Other churches offer a simpler resource table with recommended reading and other enriching material, while the ministry center of some churches houses a larger selection of resources.

- Don't leave compassion ministries on your "wish list" either. Consider partnering with faith-based organizations, community social services, and other churches to fulfill benevolent goals. In the absence of church kitchen facilities, members of Occoquan Bible Church regularly cook meals in their homes to serve at the county homeless shelter.

- Partner with other churches for certain programs. Some churches with buildings will be happy to let a Nomadic Church use their space for a program when their building isn't being used. The cost is usually minimal. Others go further. For example, Trinity Community Church and Belcroft Bible Church (http://home.att.net/~belcroftbiblechurch) combined their midweek AWANA program on Belcroft's campus. They shared the workloads, and both churches agreed that their program strengthened because of their unified efforts.

- To minimize program staffing strains that arise from the rental situation, many ministries use a rotating division of labor. If a role in a particular ministry requires transporting more than a small amount of supplies or equipment, then only ask families with sufficiently large vehicles (e.g., minivans) to help. Churches should also designate at least one storage bin or rolling cabinet per class or program, resulting in less storage and transportation stress for program volunteers.

- To ensure the longevity of programs held in rental sites, clean up and rearrange the space back to its original configuration before you leave. It helps to assign somebody like a ministry director or facility coordinator to ensure this has been done. A note of appreciation or other meaningful acknowledgment should be the only thing left behind!

- As virtually all growing Nomadic Churches do, we suggest you rent office space. The leaders we spoke to say that the more room you can afford, the better. That's why several have graduated from a simple office to a larger suite or "ministry center." In addition to providing a place for staff to accomplish all that regularly happens in an office, such a place often becomes the "nerve center" of the church. Some churches, like New Hope in Oahu, find that it's less expensive to purchase a property just for training and office space than to continue to rent it. Among the activities that can be held in such a facility are youth and singles meetings, music and drama practices, men's breakfasts, all sorts of training courses, various Bible studies and support groups, leadership and ministry committee meetings, prayer meetings, smaller community and outreach events, resource rooms, church orientation courses, homeschool events, visitor receptions, and counseling. "We definitely get our money's worth out of it," says Pastor Phil Bryant of Grace Community Church (www.grace-church.ca) in Mississauga, Ontario, in reference to their recently upgraded office center.

- Programs need guidelines for "office etiquette." If there are ample rooms at the ministry center, allow at least the priority programs to make semipermanent modifications to the space. If multiple ministries use the same areas, don't allow any one ministry to leave its mark to the detriment of the others. An updated "room use schedule" helps groups reserve space and arrange the area to be ready for the next group when they leave. Also track distribution of entrance and room keys for security.

- Just as Israel, Christ, and the early church did, value the home as a central place for spiritual learning and ministry operations.

Most of the things done at a church office, as well as other meetings (breakfasts, open houses, holiday parties, ministry meetings, baptisms, elder meetings, and so forth), can easily take place in the intimate setting of members' homes. A prime example is the network of small groups that meet weekly in homes spread throughout Nomadic Churches' target area and beyond. Every timeless biblical purpose can be accomplished in these community groups. With a homeward orientation, no church is truly a "homeless church"! (A word of caution: Even when space becomes available, continue with home groups because they are essential to effective ministry in today's world.)

- Be selective in the types of ministries you offer. Don't try to do too much too soon or feel the need to do all of the "regular" church programs. Instead, focus on the major things that fulfill your mission and lead to critical mass. Jeff Carroll of Trinity Community Church advises that a new church "avoid elaborate programming." Another lead pastor, Mike Breaux of Canyon Ridge Christian Church (www.canyonridge.org) in Las Vegas, Nevada, admitted, "Every initial staff member experienced a 'mini' crash after a while, and the fatigue level of many others in the church was too high. . . . We probably started too many ministries too quickly. . . . It didn't cross our minds that a [young] church shouldn't be tackling all that we were."[1]

These and other facility-related responses come with sacrifice, but as Bruce Johnson of Seneca Creek Community Church reflected, "There is value in letting people pay the price. The [nomadic] context offers an irreplaceable experience of struggles and inconveniences."

Equip the Program

Whatever obstacles effective Nomadic Churches face, they find a way to equip their programs adequately. We'll share some tips here. You should also review the "portability" and "storage" sections in chapter 5 for other ideas that can simplify equipment complexities.

- Wherever you hold a program, leave as much equipment there as the host will allow. Although the costs vary widely, the ability to do this is so important that churches without it agree that they'd pay extra to have it.

- If the rental site has equipment that you could use, persistently and politely make that need known to the host. The better your relationship, the greater the chance you'll get to use it. Remember, the squeaky wheel gets the grease.

- When rental equipment fails, notify the appropriate person immediately. Store their number in your cell phone, and don't be afraid to call. You're paying them for that equipment.

- Designate at least one storage bin for critical spare parts and replacement supplies like projector bulbs, power cords, and batteries. Stock a generous supply of a Nomadic Church's best friend—duct tape.

- If you don't have access to a copy machine at or near the rental site, consider bringing an inexpensive portable photocopier for making those inevitable last minute duplications. Teachers and musicians will beam with joy!

- Charge program leaders with the responsibility to store, transport, arrange, and break down at least a portion of their own equipment. Encourage them to delegate some of the duty to program participants. This taps into the resources of those most motivated to see their program succeed and lightens the overall burden by spreading it around.

- Rather than renting the meeting site again and setting up technical equipment to teach a new person how to use it, value on-the-job training—even if it takes a little longer to get a new person up to speed. It saves money, and it's a better way to train.

- Use a quick and readily decipherable wiring schematic for audiovisual equipment so that it can be easily plugged in and unhooked. As The River Church Community in San Jose, California (www.theriver.org), discovered, quick connector technology, multi-pin connectors, color-coded wires, and "cheat sheets" to map the wiring process save time, training, and problems.[2] (See appendix C for more information about portable sound systems.)

- To reduce time retrieving and setting up worship team equipment for midweek practices, store the equipment wherever they practice during the week (e.g., the church office). Some churches schedule practices before or after the Sunday service while the equipment is already on site and set up. This is also a prime opportunity to train new recruits on audiovisual equipment (sound, projection, lighting, taping) and to rehearse for dramatic sketches.

- Capitalize on the advantages of having portable equipment and experience. For example, since worship teams can take their entire system on the road with comparative ease, the music ministries of many Nomadic Churches perform periodically at community events, coffee houses, and the like. "It's pretty much like a normal Sunday morning," said one band member in reference to when their talented group called Road Show performs off site.

- If you can't adequately equip a program, don't do it! The beauty of a *mission* is that there's always another *method* to carry it out. Brainstorm options and do one wholeheartedly, rather than offer an anemic program that reflects poorly on your purpose.

- Sometimes less is better. In other words, it's fine to offer some programs that aren't encumbered with hoards of supplies and equipment. Participants may even find the simplicity refreshing and rewarding in our technology-saturated age.

Secure the People, Property, and Premises

As churches become more sensitized to security issues, stringent measures are being implemented across the country. Here are several suggestions of particular relevance to Nomadic Churches because of the concerns raised in the previous chapter.

- Don't deny that there are security and safety issues. Terrible possibilities exist today, and the first step to preventing them is acknowledging they exist.

- Carefully examine every room for potentially unsafe conditions each time you set up. If you notice anything problematic, remedy it before people arrive. For example, if a class meets in the upper level of a gymnasium that has an open pipe railing system, design some kind of barricade you can strap to the pipes to prevent little ones from climbing through and falling to the floor. Remember also to inspect any playground equipment on the campus before allowing children to use it.

- Use orange cones and signs to identify any potential hazard, including slippery floors, unfinished repairs, loose handrails, uneven sidewalks, or other defects that might cause injury.

- Make sure that cleaning chemicals and closets that contain them are locked when children are in the building. This is especially important in schools, since custodians often clean a part of the facility the church is not using. Kitchens should also be secured to prevent children from entering them.

- Stock at least one clearly labeled first-aid kit in a facility box, and make sure leaders know where it is. Maintain an updated list of medical personnel in your congregation, and immediately provide aid to an injured person if necessary. Of course, call 911 for any potentially serious injury.

- Enlist "security (hall) monitors," whose responsibility it is to roam the facility and attend to security matters. At some churches this is the sole responsibility of a few volunteers. At others, the greeters, ushers, leaders, teachers, and facility servants all share this role. Whoever does it, make sure they know what to look for (e.g., the suspicious behavior of teens in an unused portion of a high school) and what to do if anything

101

abnormal is detected (e.g., have two men approach the questionable situation together). Walkie-talkies, like those some facility crews use at larger sites, can double for security patrols. (On congregational protection, also see "Hanna" in appendix A.)

- Train all church leaders to introduce themselves politely to people they don't recognize and exchange names. It's a good practice by itself, but it will also discourage potential perpetrators from feeling they have free rein at the facility.

- Churches meeting in higher crime areas sometimes have a person patrol the parking lot once or twice during services and other events. In the evening, people should only leave a facility in pairs if the parking lot is not adequately lit.

- To prevent theft, label church equipment and lock it up securely when it's not in use. Never leave it out and unattended at the rental site.

- Develop customized picture identification badges to indicate who is a legitimate children's volunteer. The proliferation of digital cameras and lamination services has made this easier and more affordable than ever.

- Make sure that everyone who volunteers to work with minors first undergoes a thorough screening process complete with references and a criminal background check. Predators may *think* they can easily infiltrate a Nomadic Church. Make sure they can't! (Visit www.churchworkerscreening.com and www.churchvolunteercentral.com for a professional way to do this at an economical rate.)

- To prevent abductions and non-custodial parents from snatching a child, establish an identification system that ensures the person dropping off a child is the same person who picks up the child. Having numbered tags for the child and parent, taking a picture of the child and parent(s) together, or having parents leave their driver licenses are the most common methods.

- Limit those allowed to enter the nursery to pre-screened workers. Even parents should not be allowed in. To regulate this screening, it's best to have only one main entrance. Gates should keep babies and toddlers safely in their separate areas and keep others out. If necessary, improvise some form of barrier system (try using dividers or stable storage cabinets) around the children's area.

- Classrooms for young children should not be located adjacent to facility exits, so that children do not "escape" and intruders do not enter.

- Lock or ask the host to lock all doors the church does not use before or while you're meeting. Have a responsible person (e.g., a hall monitor) ensure that this has been done each week. Unless the doors open from the inside, make sure there are still adequate escape routes in case of emergency.

- Always have at least two adults attend to a group of young children. Children should never be left alone while a volunteer takes a child to the bathroom.

- If an outside group uses part of your meeting site (e.g., a basketball team in a school gym), request that they only use the entrance closest to their area. This will inhibit outsiders from intermingling with children in the halls and make them more conspicuous if they try.

- If there are no fire extinguishers, buy several and periodically test them. Make sure all leaders know the placement of the extinguishers.

- If there are no emergency plans posted, either draw a plan up yourselves or insist the host do so (it's legally required of public facilities). Then post evacuation diagrams in conspicuous places around the facility and update them if the configuration of the facility changes. Include emergency contact numbers right on the diagrams.

- If a malfunctioning fire alarm system rings during a meeting, seize it as an opportunity to practice your emergency escape route. Later, make sure the host knows what happened.

Although nothing is entirely foolproof, these types of measures go a long way toward providing a secure experience during programs and services. Don't join the ranks of church leaders who regret taking a shortcut!

Responses to Special Event Challenges

Because special events are a valued and vibrant part of their ministry, effective Nomadic Churches aggressively respond to the many facility-induced limitations, inconveniences, and struggles they face when conducting (or not being able to conduct) special church events. Since many of the responses to physical, personnel, and program challenges apply equally to special event challenges, we will focus only on *new* information that helps overcome event impediments and inconveniences.

"Without a doubt the biggest challenge we face in renting school facilities is finding a facility large enough to accommodate large gatherings on a day other than Sunday." —Joe Carmichael, Pastor of Community of Hope UMC (www.communityofhope.com), Mansfield, Texas

- Weddings are usually solved by making some form of alternative, off-site arrangements. A healthy networking relationship with an established church can translate into practical utility— borrowing the church building. Other times, no church building need be involved. In either case, enlisting a wedding coordinator who is (or can become) familiar with a wedding facility will make the experience far less stressful for everyone.

- Nomadic Churches hold baptisms just about anywhere there's water (of course, those who practice modes of baptism other than immersion have an easier time with this).[3] Some prefer rivers, lakes, bays, or the ocean for their "natural feel." Others use private pools or other church buildings. Churches often alternate sites depending on the outdoor temperature, the availability of a site, and the size of the event. Some prefer a public setting like the pool of a YMCA because of the additional witnessing opportunities the ceremony provides. Chesapeake Christian Fellowship (www.4theLord.org) in Davidsonville, Maryland, just built a building but still plans to hold baptisms in the same outdoor spa they grew accustomed to as a portable church because of how meaningful the place became to them. Members of New Hope Christian Fellowship look forward to a festive luau on the beach whenever they hold baptisms.

- Memorial services are generally held in a funeral home chapel or another church's building. These services have even been held in a natural outdoor setting when doing so was befitting to the deceased and desired by the family.

- Extra-large events can be accomplished by renting a larger building or outdoor stadium or facility in the area. Some churches team with multiple churches in the area to offer high impact community events in which each church shares some of the cost and work.

- Summer children's programs (like Vacation Bible Schools) don't have to be held on a church campus. In fact, it may be better to go *to* the kids with programs like Sidewalk Sunday School or Child Evangelism Fellowship's Good News Clubs that can meet in parks, community children's centers, or members' backyards.[4]

- Fellowship dinners are sometimes held at a banquet facility, restaurant, or the school cafeteria after services. Potlucks, catering, going out, and ordering in compensate for the lack of church kitchen facilities. Indoor and outdoor park and recreation facilities are also commonly used for various fellowship and outreach picnics and events.

- Sports leagues, clinics, and recreational tournaments can be held at various outdoor and indoor community locations.

- Go out of your way to establish good relationships with other community groups. When Occoquan Bible Church was told their school would be remodeled during the summer along with half of the other schools in the county, Pastor Kyle Austin called the local Boys and Girls Club that they had rented for special events annually. To Austin's delight, the director told him another church had also called that day, but she would "take care" of Occoquan because they were "regulars."

- Don't overlook the importance of small events. Jeff Carroll, senior pastor of Trinity Community Church, suggests Nomadic Churches "nurture the intimacy factor." Bigger is not always better.

- Special events require not only planning far ahead for the event but also for the facility and other obstacles. Rather than be discouraged, take advantage of this extra time to prepare to execute a great event.

- Check out all equipment in *advance* of the event. If you plan to use on-site equipment, make sure it's there and in working condition before the event, rather than solely relying on the word of the host.

- Hold practices and rehearsals anywhere you can before renting the facilities again. You may have to improvise a bit. One director built a platform in an empty garage to make a rehearsal place. Another church uses dramas that are comprised exclusively of smaller acts. This allows groups to practice in small areas and to come together for only one full rehearsal.

- Hire specialized help as needed. For example, some churches employ a professional media technician to help them with their large holiday productions. The cost is usually far less than moving the production to a facility with more sophisticated equipment.

- The holidays shouldn't be ho-hum in a Nomadic Church. Create a decorations team to perform enhancements especially for holidays and other all-church events. This is often part of a facility crew or just a subcommittee of a women's ministry or worship team.

- If the facilities aren't large enough, hold the special event more than once. Multiple nights reduce parking problems, give people a choice of times, and keep the crowd smaller for better interaction with newcomers.

- Don't filter out what you *think* is impossible. Approach special events as if anything is possible. Filtering out what you think is impossible usually leads to filtering out more than is necessary.

In the previous chapter, we quoted Kent Husted saying he mentally sifts out programs and events he'd like to do but can't. This successful youth pastor continued, however, "You can't dwell on it. Plus there's always something you *can* do." That "can do" attitude pervades the leadership of effective Nomadic Churches. The proof is in their excellent programs and events— and especially the lives changed by those ministries!

Talk Time for Teams

For Pre-Plant Teams

- Are you all absolutely committed to not allowing your rental status to deter you from accomplishing the ministries that are critical to fulfilling your mission? Draft a resolution, explain it to every leader, and have them sign it.

- What programs do you agree you do *not* need to start in the formative period of your church? Why?

- With the list you developed in the last chapter of the priority programs and special events you'd like to do in the first year, think of where you might hold them. Brainstorm as many potential rentable or free sites as possible. Begin to prioritize and contact these places to make sure the space is suitable, affordable, and available.

- List who you might be able to partner with in your target area to offset facility and program challenges. Consider (a) other mobile churches; (b) churches with buildings; and (c) community service organizations. Begin contacting their leaders and lay the foundation for a mutually beneficial relationship.

- Where will your office space(s) be located? What should you look for in this space, if not now, a little down the road?

- Discuss what roles the home will play in your new church. What are some spiritual, relational, and practical benefits of this arrangement?

- What do you need to do to provide a secure and safe environment for your services, programs, and events?

- If you've reached out to a more experienced Nomadic Church for guidance, see what tactics you can glean from them in dealing with your own program and event challenges.

- Does your anticipated approach to ministry need to be adjusted in order to carry out the responses offered above?

- In addition to what we've offered, what else might you do to prevent or lessen the impact of program challenges raised in the previous chapter? Special event challenges?

For Post-Plant Teams

- Have you, because of your rental status, given up on offering a certain ministry that is critical to your mission? Why? What can you do to reverse that poisonous trend and advance your mission? Are you running programs or events that you really don't *need* to offer? Could the resources going to these be diverted to a priority ministry that is presently suffering?

- What aesthetic enhancements and space redistributions have you made and could you make to create a more suitable environment for programs and events?

- If you do not have an office space or ministry center, how might it benefit you? If you do, how has it benefited you? How might you better use that space?

- How have homes factored into your ministry? How can they be used even more? What benefits can result? Any challenges?

- Is there a way to handle your "equipment complexities" better?

- What are you doing to provide a secure and safe environment during your services, programs, and events? How can you improve even more?

- Have you thought about adopting a younger Nomadic Church in your area yet? When you do, share your experience in handling program and event challenges—and listen to their ideas.

- In addition to what we've offered, what else have you done to prevent or lessen the impact of program challenges like those raised in the previous chapter? Special event challenges?

- Which of the suggestions above or others you have thought of will you implement to help prevent or alleviate your facility-related program and event challenges? Who will be responsible to do so? What is the timeline for beginning and evaluating these new measures?

CHAPTER EIGHT

REVEALING VISITOR AND FINANCIAL CHALLENGES

Without nickels and noses," an old preacher explained to a group of bright-eyed church planters, "you ain't got a church!" He does have a point. Churches constantly in short supply of people and money are usually on their way out. It's not that the two are equally important, but a church does need to raise and release both disciples and dollars. Barriers to one tend to hinder the other in the contemporary American church. In this chapter we will explore facility-related challenges Nomadic Churches face in regard to reaching and retaining visitors and to financial matters.

Visitor Challenges

One of our research objectives was to determine whether growing Nomadic Churches actually experience noticeable visitor challenges. We found that they do. However, the core churches in our study range from 250 average worshipers per week to more than ten thousand, and none show signs of reaching a permanent plateau or exhausting their growth potential. So the question isn't *whether* Nomadic Churches add to their constituency, but rather how facility-related matters complicate their efforts to reach and retain more people for Christ. The challenges we discovered can be divided into two subcategories: (1) external opinions and (2) internal obstacles.

A visitor challenge refers to any mild to severe inability to attract or retain individuals due to something related to being a Nomadic Church.

External Opinions

Theological matters aside for the moment, opinions are everything when it comes to whether a person—Christian or not—decides to visit a particular church. Nomadic leaders believe that personal relationships are the primary, though not exclusive, means by which the majority of visitors are introduced to their churches. Even so, whether persons visit and return is partly dependent on their opinion of the inviter and the church to which they are invited. The same holds true for any form of marketing.

Most people have some perception of what a church ought to look like. Often rented facilities do not live up to those perceptions, making it harder to reach certain visitors than it is for a church with its own facilities.

Although we expected respondents to report that they have noticed at least a few mild negative perceptions from some folk in the community, the responses were stronger than we anticipated. Leaders have more than casually heard and sensed that some people have not visited their church because of something traceable to meeting in rented facilities. As one pastor explained, "Some just feel weird about meeting in a school, including some seekers, because everyone has some expectations of what a church is—what it should look like." A different pastor said, "They ask, 'Is this thing permanent or fly-by-night?'" Another reasoned, "Many [people] want a building to establish you as a legitimate church. It's the whole 'psychology of permanence' that we're up against," which he explained as the feeling of security and stability that people derive from being linked to stable fixtures like church buildings. These responses may be even truer for reaching those with a "high church, liturgical background" for whom a church isn't a church without a church building. The pastor of a church that targets such people shared, "It can be a disaster when they find out we meet in a school."

One pastor told us he recently fielded an inquiry about his church from a lady who was not an "experienced Christian." As they talked, though, she seemed interested—maybe even excited—about the church and the ministries geared toward her and her two children. She wanted to visit! Then came her innocent question about where the church meets. The pastor's answer, "Woodbridge Middle School," was met with a deafening moment of silence. What went through her mind in those few seconds? Perhaps it was something we've already discussed—or maybe something mentioned below.

A particular meeting site may not only inaccurately reflect the church, it may even betray its real mission, membership, or ministry.

Perceptions of instability can be even more intense toward newer Nomadic Churches because they don't have a long track record to point to as proof of their permanence. This sensitivity can also extend to the leadership, as one pastor shared: "Some doubted the commitment of the pastoral staff to a church without a permanent structure." Early on a few people actually told him they would not visit the church because they questioned whether the church or its staff would persevere.

As soon as some visit these churches "they're interested right away in when we're going to build," says one pastor. Another pastor believes that "more 'experienced Christians' know a building campaign is coming and don't want anything to do with that." People have told some pastors that they would not visit or return to the church because they did not want to have to go through the portable church experience—or endure it again. Others may be glad to tag along for a while but without making serious time or financial commitments until they know the church is going to survive long-term. In their minds, that may be indicated by building plans.

The lack of a building also means there's one less way for a church to communicate its intended "image" to the community. A particular meeting site may not only inaccurately reflect the church, it may even betray its real mission, membership, or ministry. The effect is only compounded by the wide variety of quarters in which Nomadic Churches are housed (see table 4 in chapter 9). Some places are better than others, but none compare to the fully equipped modern church buildings that dot the landscape of many American communities.

Internal Obstacles

In addition to the impact of outsiders' negative or naive opinions, Nomadic Churches must cope with internal facility-related obstacles to retaining visitors. Perhaps most painful is when an attendee suggests or implies that the church is "less than" other churches or "incomplete" because the church doesn't have its own building. More common than encountering this "inferiority perception" is for leaders to hear that some visitors left or did not return to their church because they don't have their own building or because of something that is traceable to meeting in a certain rented facility.

"Those responsible for the real estate may have a tremendous impact on how many people appear for Sunday morning worship." —Lyle Schaller[1]

The facility-related reasons certain people do not attend or new attendees do not return to a particular Nomadic Church are as varied as the many challenges already raised in this book. If the host will not allow signs to be strategically posted for maximum drive-by visibility, not to mention permanently posted at the meeting site, some who might otherwise be made aware of the church will miss it. If construction or cleaning by the host inconveniences attendees or shuts down all or part of the facility, a person might be deterred from visiting or returning. If foul odors, crowded rooms, disheveled landscaping, parking problems, dirty or cluttered facilities, inappropriately sized furnishings, inadequate restrooms, or an uncomfortable climate affect the church, they can also repel those newly investigating the church. Since Christmas and Easter are times that schools are often in extra disarray, a percentage of visitors might be turned off during these critical outreach seasons.

Other issues stemming from challenges already mentioned also deserve discussion here. Since it is sometimes overwhelming even for regular attendees to navigate the facility to find classrooms, to a first-time visitor it may feel as intimidating as a high-school freshman's first day of school. If audiovisual barriers, aesthetic shortcomings, distracting "sanctuaries," and related limitations prevent the church from attaining its desired professionalism, the results may factor into a visitor's decision not to return. Some leaders say it is for many of these reasons that certain congregants would invite more people to visit the church if it met in its own building.

When there are perceived shortcomings in security, safety, or children's accommodations—even if just for a brief time—some parents "feel insecure," according to one pastor. A few periodically leave for such reasons. Sudden facility moves can also result in a measure of attrition, because some who wish to visit may not be aware of the change, and it may take a while for word to spread about the new meeting place. Plus, some may consider the new location to be just far enough away to discontinue or forego attendance. Bay Area Fellowship (www.bayareafellowship.org) in Corpus Christi, Texas, moved from its own facility to a larger rented facility only five miles away and attendance dropped from 2,500 to 1,800 in one week. The church returned to its previous site and six months later was running 3,300 in worship.

The degree to which a meeting place prevents people from thinking, "I belong here; people care about me," is the degree to which some numerical growth is hindered.

114

A significant frustration for some church staff is feeling too rushed by rental time constraints to interact sufficiently with visitors. Curtains, carpets, and cribs roaring through halls and lobbies do not help matters. Key leaders sometimes mingle less with visitors because they have to be task-oriented just to get ready for services and then to break down. For some churches there are facility-imposed limitations on how much spontaneous fellowship and relational interaction can happen on Sunday morning. The lack of a large lobby or other space to informally congregate is often the culprit. New Life Christian Church chose to move to a new site because, as their executive minister Todd Wilson explained, their old "rental facility was designed to get people in and out, not to get them to connect after services."

Due to facility obstacles, we have seen that certain evangelistic and benevolent venues have been shelved for the time being. Churches wanting to begin a new service, such as a Saturday evening outreach venue, have to consider the multiple obstacles that will confront them. One pastor recognized that "many outreach events need a large-group context," which they and some other Nomadic Churches have difficulty offering due to space limitations. Whenever a program or event that could attract or assimilate new attendees must be scrapped due to facility issues, some people may not connect with Christ or the existing congregants.

How much more Nomadic Churches might grow without these facility-induced external opinions and internal obstacles is unknown. But their presence is quite clear. And they leave some members and leaders longing for the day they settle into their own building.

Financial Challenges

Money may not make the world go 'round, but it sure does keep the lights on. From its inception, the church has rarely enjoyed financial excess. There are simply too many needs in this world and too many ways limited funds can be allotted to meet them. Accordingly, every church faces some degree of financial stress.

Even though the core churches in our study have annual

operating budgets that far exceed the national average, they too have strains. The question here, however, is not whether successful Nomadic Churches spend money or could use more of it, but what financial challenges do they face that can be partly or largely attributed to the fact that they are a homeless church. We've found several and will discuss examples with the aid of two categories: (1) ongoing expenses and (2) occasional expenses.

Financial challenges refer to mild to severe stresses, burdens, or complications of a financial nature related to or resulting from a church's portable status.

Ongoing Expenses

Despite their fiscal health, leaders agree that their churches face extra and unique financial expenses because they are a Nomadic Church. Strain comes from the ongoing financial outlay for rental costs while compensating staff, funding programs, and saving (or already paying) for future land on which to build.

Renting is usually a tremendous financial asset (see the next chapter), but some leaders single out facility rental costs as the prime source of financial strain. Although there are better bargains, it's not unknown for Nomadic Churches to pay over $1,500 per week just for the Sunday space. The larger and nicer the facility and the bigger the church (not to mention the more venues or portable campuses it may have), the higher the cost. Rates also increase the closer one gets to a suburban/urban area and the more services, programs, and events a church offers. Competition from other Nomadic Churches and community groups can force a church into the most costly rental sites. There are probably more outrageous figures, but one church we studied in the Washington, D.C., area pays over $10,000 per month just for its Sunday morning rental space. The senior pastor muses, "That would make a healthy mortgage payment."

For sure, the majority of Nomadic Churches would pay more for a building of their own than they do a rental facility. "The rub," explains one business administrator, "is what we get—or don't get—for the money we spend." Nomadic Church facilities are like apartment living. There are advantages to this housing situation, but there is also no ownership of the space or the many benefits that come along with that privilege—professional upkeep, sufficient storage, permanent aesthetic enhancements, ease of scheduling, structural reconfiguration, space for multiple groups every day, and so forth.

Liability insurance can also be more expensive, because it must cover the church in multiple rental sites. Proof of coverage must be presented along with each rental contract, so a comprehensive policy must be in hand before seeking to rent a public facility. Offsite storage also costs additional money. At least one church pays more than twice as much for its storage each month than they do for their part-time facility coordinator!

Growing Nomadic Churches also rent separate office space, which is subject to the same factors that increase worship space rent. When an office suite is abandoned in favor of establishing a larger ministry center (such as at a strip mall or warehouse), a large church's total financial outlay for rental facilities could flirt with the half-million-dollar mark per year. Fortunately, it is not essential that a church spend anywhere near this much to be effective, and certainly very few do. But some Nomadic Churches may find that they spend as much (and occasionally more) on their total facilities as churches with buildings spend.[2] As a couple of pastors and accountants pointed out, mortgages can be fixed or refinanced at a lower rate. But rental rates only increase—and usually annually. Adding staff while aggressively saving for future facilities can compound the strain of ongoing expenses. And it can really get tough in the span when a church begins paying monthly for its land without shedding any of its other rental costs.

Occasional Expenses

The ongoing expenses might be less burdensome if there were not a whole range of additional expenses arising from a church's portable status. Although these extra financial expenses occur only once or sporadically, unlike those above that are payable weekly or monthly, they add up.

Capital expenditures can be hefty. Although it may pay off down the road, the outlay for services from a nomadic-friendly organization like Portable Church Industries can cost hundreds of thousands of dollars for large churches. Multiple rolling cabinets, sophisticated multimedia systems, transportation trucks, and trailers are expensive. Although one executive pastor says he "would have preferred to spend money elsewhere," he acknowledged these tools are "essential to our ministry." Churches also pay when theft and vandalism plague transportation vehicles and their contents when there is no totally secure place to park them.

More space requires more money. Expenses for additional space are incurred any time there is a need for an extra classroom, a gym for a sports tournament, a cafeteria or a banquet hall for a dinner, a community center for a concert or conference, a park for a special event, a public pool for a baptism, an auditorium for events and practices, and so on. The rental rate for a "Special Use Permit" to use a site outside of the regular contract period may be higher than the normal rental cost. When the time allotted is exceeded, even due to unforeseen circumstances, the host can assess a financial penalty. On the flip side, when all or part of the facility is shut down due to something like a renovation or custodial mishap, the church may not be reimbursed for the unused space. Leaders also sometimes feel an underlying "pressure" to substantially compensate the host and its personnel beyond what they contractually owe.

Essentially everything the church needs must be portable, and sometimes mobile equipment is more expensive.

The cost for various pieces of equipment, while not overwhelming by itself, adds up. Portable sound systems, projectors and projection screens, laptops for audiovisual support, TV/VCR combinations, cooling fans, and freestanding lights are examples. Even portable overhead projectors still cost more than their larger cousins. Moreover, to use some on-site equipment, if even available, requires payment. One of the resulting dilemmas is deciding what to buy and not to buy, because some equipment purchased by a church may have little or no use in a future rented or permanent facility.

Every nomadic leader also notes that "stuff breaks more." The continual shifting of equipment takes its toll. We could tell many stories but one should suffice. During a visit we saw a church's video projector fall off its platform, breaking its $900 bulb. Rarely would that happen in a church building, where it would have been secured in a stationary spot. Later that same morning, we witnessed a power cord wrap around the wheel of a cart being pushed through the lobby. Down came the top layer, including a pair of speakers. And these examples come from one of the better organized and equipped churches we've seen!

A Nomadic Church's equipment gets as much wear and tear as the servants who tend to it.

Without even mentioning the astronomical amount needed to purchase land and prepare to build on it, other facility-related expenses drain the budget. These include portable staging, a portable pulpit and communion table, durable indoor and outdoor signs, age-appropriate furnishings, curtain frames and dividers, portable cribs, lightweight cleaning equipment, carpets and padding, storage bins, literature and display racks, backdrops, an endless stream of duct tape, facility-related legal costs, and various site-specific aesthetic enhancements. While every church buys most of these items, they are often used up or worn out quicker by a Nomadic Church and may be of little or no value in a future building or rental site. Other minor supplies, like the bathroom provisions some churches bring on site, are only frustrating because it seems they should be covered by the rental fees.

As we've seen, effective Nomadic Churches are willing to expend money—and a lot of other things—in order to prevent and respond to their facility-related challenges. How they do so when it comes to visitor and financial challenges is the subject of the next chapter.

Talk Time for Teams

For Pre-Plant Teams

- What facility-related visitor challenges have surfaced in this chapter that you may not have considered before? Financial challenges? Can you think of others you might face?

- Are you spiritually and emotionally prepared for the "external opinions" some will have of you and your church? Role play some possible responses you could make when you hear them expressed by people in the community or in your church.

- How does this information have an impact on the kind of rental facilities you seek to secure for church services, programs, and events? Compare two or more possible rental sites with the eyes of a visitor. What potential barriers are there to maximizing your attraction and retention of visitors? Potential advantages? Do a cost-benefit analysis of each site.

- If you haven't, begin the process of obtaining comprehensive liability insurance so that you can rent a public site.

- Are you prepared for the financial challenges of operating a Nomadic Church? How will you prepare? Take some time to write a master list of everything you anticipate needing to buy (or acquire somehow) within the first year (for ideas see www.church-planting.net). Prioritize the capital expenditures (big-ticket items) within your master budget.

- Does this chapter alter your attitude or values toward visitor attraction and retention and/or church finances?

For Post-Plant Teams

- Which facility-related challenges described in this chapter can you identify with? Share your stories and perspectives with each other.

- What other examples of facility-related visitor challenges could you add to what's presented above? Financial challenges?

- How have you handled the "external opinions" some have of you as a Nomadic Church? How could you better respond when they come up in the future?

- Thinking with the mind of an outsider, what barriers might your current rental site(s) present to attracting and retaining every possible visitor? What "internal obstacles" have you already removed? How will you minimize the impact of others?

- Calculate the total amount you spend on facilities in a year—the worship site, program and special event sites, office rent and utilities, insurance, transportation, storage, host gifts, etc. Compared to the figure in the endnotes, do you spend a higher or lower percentage on facilities than the average American church? What difference, if any, does this make to you?

- How do this chapter and your discussion affect your thinking, feelings, attitudes, values, and actions toward:
    those in the community,
    those in your church,
    your finances,
    your meeting site(s), and
    your future plans?

CHAPTER NINE

RESPONDING TO VISITOR AND FINANCIAL CHALLENGES

Rather than wallow in limitations and wither in attendance, effective Nomadic Churches tackle facility-induced visitor and financial challenges with as much gusto as they combat the myriad of other challenges that confront them. Their healthy inclusion of new faces and intake of new finances bear irrefutable testimony to those efforts. Just how this momentum is sustained above the norm, despite the lack of permanent housing, is the subject of this chapter. In keeping with our purpose we don't intend to give general church growth or financial advice. But we do hope this information will help you overcome facility-related obstacles that can sap your growth in terms of people or money.

"Your first step in doing the will of God is to try your best to do it with the least dependence on money. Instead of going to money, use imagination and resourcefulness. 'If I had more building, more staff, more money. . . .' This line of reasoning is endless. For Easter rent the stadium, and it takes the church into the marketplace. By going to the marketplace people are coming to Christ. Let's take the money we would put into mortgage and

put it into ministry."—Wayne Cordeiro,
Pastor of New Hope Christian Fellowship

Responses to Visitor Challenges

All the core churches in our study have grown at least 500 percent since their inception, some well over 5000 percent! And they continue to add to their congregation, some modestly and some voraciously. While there is great diversity in their actual size, these figures far exceed the average church growth rate in the U.S. So let's consider some tactics that have helped them respond to their facility-related visitor challenges. We will use the same two categories from chapter 8.

Responses to External Opinions

The leaders of growing Nomadic Churches initiate several strategies to minimize the negative impressions that we have seen some people have of them.

- Virtually every Nomadic Church highly values strategic marketing. Their goal is to make the church more "tangible" *to* the community and "visible" *in* the community. Bill Cornelius, pastor of Bay Area Fellowship, remarked: "My goal was for it to be impossible for anyone in our city to be unaware of Bay Area." This is reflected by the higher than average amount of money they and churches like them allocate to various forms of marketing. Kurt Oheim, pastor of Pinnacle Church in Amarillo, Texas (www.sayingyes.com), knows the value of advertising: "Every Saturday on my five-mile run I take a different route so I can put door knockers on houses as I walk back home."

- Create a polished corporate image. A recognizable slogan and distinct logo that you constantly use can reinforce an impression of stability and identity in people's minds. (Several resources in appendix A will help a church upgrade its image.)

- Creative and professional informational brochures and advertisement campaigns can lend a sense of credibility and permanence and lessen hesitancies certain people have about visiting. However, keep in mind that some churches found that their early "slick advertising campaigns" were counter-productive to visitor retention, because they did not realistically represent the church and its accommodations. Bruce Johnson of Seneca Creek Community Church gives a key piece of advice to new Nomadic Churches: "Under sell and over deliver!"

- In addition to the benefits we've mentioned, securing an office suite or ministry center in the geographical target area offers some ongoing visibility, provides a nonresidential mailing address, adds a semblance of stability, and affords a place for focused visitor attraction and retention efforts (e.g., guest receptions and church orientation courses). The higher the public visibility, the better, because leaders also report that people discover their churches from seeing the office.

- As soon as you own any property, erect quality signage on it. A professional sign boldly announces, "We're here to stay!" If you're not able to leave it up permanently, then make it portable. Keep it simple but display the church name, logo, Web site address, phone number, a key corporate statement (e.g., your vision statement), and where and when the church currently meets. Similar signs outside your office suite, on your transportation vehicles and trailers, and around your storage site(s) deliver some of the same impact. Signs are "one of the quickest, most economical ways to create an identity,"[1] and there are many people in Nomadic Churches today who "accidentally" drove by such signs.

- Capitalize on your virtual presence.[2] An attractive, informative, and professional church Web site can build a tangible bridge to the community. This is a major reason growing Nomadic Churches report that they highly value their Internet exposure and give it great attention. See appendix D for essential qualities of Nomadic Church Web sites.

- Decentralize deliberately. When seeking to overcome the skeptical opinions of some in the community, little rivals the impact of being *in* the community positively influencing it. The good news is that various facility challenges already cause Nomadic Churches to decentralize—to disperse from an area of concentration like a church building and to be out in the community where congregants can interact with those whom they are trying to reach. What remains is to embrace and champion this posture.[3] Organize community service projects, join in community events, and value the unique chance to rub shoulders with real people when you meet in various community locations. Use the church office, homes, public sites, and networking with other organizations and churches to your fullest advantage. Ultimately, make it your aim to be able to give a confident "yes" in reply to this question: "Would this community miss our church if we disappeared tomorrow?"

- Accentuate the positives of not having a traditional church building. Some people actually attend and stick *because* they like a Nomadic Church. Leaders we surveyed strongly agreed with the statement, "We have reason to believe we have reached some folks we may have otherwise not reached because of being a Nomadic Church." Each interview group offered stories of some unchurched who viewed the nontraditional church facility as "less threatening" to them. "A school is far more familiar than a church building to seekers," explained one creative communications pastor. Some who have rebelled against the institution of Christianity—of which buildings are a hallmark—prefer a mobile setting. Moreover, some transplanted Christians actually *look* for a church home in a portable church. One such member whose job relocates him frequently told us he does this "because they tend to be less facility-driven, more biblically focused and energetic." Others "like to get in on the ground floor of a newer church without a building," explained an elder at one church. (See chapter 1, table 2 for other advantages of the portable paradigm that you can capitalize upon.)

- Remain people-oriented. While there may be distractions to interaction at the rental site, experienced nomadic pastors tell

125

us that overall the lack of a building helps them "focus on people more." This, they say, translates into drawing and keeping more people. Having ample time to interact with visitors is another reason that at least key leaders should not be encumbered with the bulk of the weekly facility operations (hence, a facility coordinator position). Beyond that, every leader we interviewed agreed that a personal invitation from a church member to somebody in his or her relational web is the *most* effective recruiting tool of all.

- Do not belabor facility-related financial issues in corporate worship services. Some Christians are anxious about visiting a Nomadic Church because of fear they will automatically be sucked into a building campaign. More important, the unchurched have keen misgivings when it comes to money and the church. It is better not to confirm their suspicions and perpetually dwell on it in public services. Many Nomadic Churches tell their guests that the Sunday offering is an act of worship by their regular participants. First-time guests, on the other hand, are encouraged to relax and focus on God. Many emergent Nomadic Churches seem to favor an "offering box" approach to collect contributions, rather than passing collection receptacles during the service.

- Church leaders in ineffective Nomadic Churches have a tendency to fall victim to the "we're just gonna stay a small church" syndrome. Don't ever allow this attitude to rear its ugly head. The moment you hear it or feel it, kill it quickly before it kills you! For instance, when you hear someone say, "If we get much bigger we won't know everyone anymore," respond, "The real question isn't do we know everyone, but does everyone in town know God?" Or when you hear someone say, "Shouldn't we take better care of who we've got before we go after anyone else?" respond, "Jesus didn't say, 'Go care for everyone.' He said, 'Go make disciples of everyone.'" Or when someone suggests, "Aren't we big enough?" respond, "The issue isn't size. The role of the church is to make disciples. If we cease doing that, we cease being the church."

- As much as visitor and other challenges may leave some members and leaders longing for their own facility, do not allow new facilities to be viewed as either the end or the primary means of ministry. A building never warrants that much importance![4]

- Stay the course. Certain stigmas that affect Nomadic Churches are quickly evaporating in our wireless world. Even the business and education communities are shifting focus away from a single, central campus mindset. The proliferation of telecommuting, business incubators in unlikely places, distance learning, telework, Internet-based training and commerce, and remote and mobile offices and project teams serve to de-emphasize place in favor of process. Mobility is becoming more normalized every year as Americans become even more accustomed to professionals and businesspeople working in nontraditional places.[5] The leftover perceptions of instability and transience that some have of mobile churches or their staff will shrink as you demonstrate otherwise.

- Focus on strong leadership, solid worship, significant fellowship, strategic outreach, and systematic discipleship. While you should always make diligent efforts to attract and retain visitors, remember to couple it with a theologically grounded trust in the *Lord's* work. He will open doors that seem sealed shut, like the ones described on the Web site of Grace Bible Church in Virginia Beach, Virginia (www.vbgbc.org): "In January of 1992 we were blessed with a miracle. The use of high schools which had been closed to churches before suddenly became a possibility. The principal of Kellam High School, Dr. Williams, practically opened his arms to us when other high schools flatly refused to talk with us. We were there until October 1994 and praise the Lord for the facility and the school's openness to us." The One who said, "I will build my church" is still in the business of building his church (Matt 16:18)!

Responses to Internal Obstacles

In addition to responding to negative and naive opinions from those outside the church, effective Nomadic Churches respond intuitively and intentionally to *internal* obstacles in order to maximize visitor attraction and retention. With the challenges of the previous chapter as our backdrop, here are some ways they do this.

- Select a strategically located meeting site. Certain obstacles can be averted by securing a visible, accessible location in the target area. This will preferably be an attractive facility near a major thoroughfare and with a good reputation in the community. According to Todd Wilson, New Life Christian Church chose the Regal Cinemas for its newest campus largely because it "has regional name recognition; anyone within 10 miles of the theater knows where it is located." Although there are limited available, adequate, and affordable meeting sites in a given geographical area, there are usually several potential places from which to choose. Table 4 offers suggestions of where to look.

- Use each move as a learning experience to upgrade your next location. Although new challenges await each place, your previous experience provides a platform to alleviate many irritating issues in the previous facility. The more a location will help you accomplish your goals, the more aggressively you should pursue it.

- When a meeting place is shut down for whatever reason on a given Sunday, post at least one church sign as normal. Station someone onsite to explain the situation to visitors and to direct them to where the morning services will be held. Start the service later than normal to allow people time to arrive. Handing out church literature, a printed map to the new meeting site, and a warm cup of coffee also helps. If the facility is terminated altogether, use the same procedure for at least a month, in addition to making immediate announcements through phone calls, e-mails, the church Web site, and media outlets.

- Announce your presence to visitors and those simply passing by. The first to arrive each Sunday morning should post large banners or sidewalk boards advertising the church. Directional signs staked in the ground at strategic intersections also raise awareness of the church. Carefully position everything so that it can be easily read by passing traffic. Backed by countless stories, nomadic pastors tell us that people will occasionally "stop in" to visit when they see a sign on their way somewhere else.

• Use signs to indicate the main entrance(s), especially if the facility has multiple entry points. It is popular to unfurl a durable banner over this entrance. This practice will keep people from using the wrong doors and allow you to concentrate your welcoming efforts at the main entrance(s).

• Provide convenient parking for guests and encourage leaders and core members not to use the spaces closest to the entrances.[6] If "Visitor Parking Only" signs are posted in front of the main entrance, as they are at most schools, ask members to respect those signs. Or, make your own "Guest Parking" signs so visitors are only a short walk from the main entrance and can be easily seen by greeters. During winter weather, these spots should be cleared entirely of ice or snow as evidence of the visitor's importance. Parking lot attendants can also greet cars with a smile, direct traffic, point visitors toward open spaces, and escort guests with umbrellas in the rain.

• Make sure the site has adequate handicapped accessibility. If there is none, work with the host to create it according to the local ordinances that govern public facilities.

• Train a team of friendly greeters who will warmly welcome people, make them feel at ease, answer their questions, and point them to where they need to go. Position some *in front of* the main doors if it is even slightly unclear which entrance guests should use to enter the facility.

• Position enticing refreshment centers and well-stocked information displays at entrances to help connect people with each other and with the church. Instead of the normal "bad" church coffee, spend the extra time and money to brew quality coffee.

Don't forget those who don't drink coffee, and please, if you provide donuts, also put out some fruit!

- Configure the site to be user-friendly. Make ample use of printed signs to clearly point people to the worship area, the nursery, restrooms, and every other room the church is using. In schools and similar sites, hang signs from ceiling tiles for better visibility down long halls. Place updated paper maps or a diagram at every entrance to help people navigate the facility, and keep as many classes as possible in the same area of the facility. This makes the facility more navigable and less confusing or intimidating to visitors.

- Show people you care. While nothing takes the place of the personal touch, even making the effort to pad nursery floors and post fire evacuation plans outside every children's room could not only save a life but whispers to a mother, "Your little girl is important to us, too." These efforts subtly communicate to visitors that you care about them and their first experiences with your church.

- Provide gifts for first-time guests. We've seen a variety, like candy-filled church coffee mugs, sermon tapes, inscribed pens, and reception packets (minus the stewardship campaign pledge card!). These can help visitors feel important and connect with another "live person" before leaving the rental site.

- Reserve an area to welcome visitors as well as to give them an opportunity after worship to register any spiritual decision they may have made that morning. These areas should allow a few leaders to focus exclusively on visitors without the whirl of distracting breakdown activities. Some create a "VIP room" with refreshments and a brief introduction to the church. Whether or not you have such an area, strive to connect in some personal way with every guest within twenty-four hours of their visit.

- Sweat the small stuff. Given the variety of facility-related stresses and Sunday surprises Nomadic Churches face, one might expect them to brush off the "details" to focus exclusively on the "big picture" of what they want to accomplish. But that's not true of growing Nomadic Churches; they "do the details." One tool used by many is a "quality control checklist" or an "excellence inspection." From laying down welcome mats to disinfecting toilet seats to positioning artificial trees, this document delineates every detail of the morning routine so that no little touch is missed. Great churches reason that every person who visits or attends is worth the time. In the process, they prove that portable doesn't have to mean pitiful!

- Be consistent with your enhancement efforts. With the constant strain, it's easy for parts of the regular setup routine to be skipped periodically. Use rotating facility teams so that a capable crew is always ready to do the job, including during peak vacation seasons and holiday weekends. After all, that may be just the week a person decides to visit or revisit your church.

- Connect with new people *outside of* the regular rental period. As important as Sunday morning efforts are, few things bear more lasting fruit than interacting with visitors in a more relational, relaxed atmosphere. That's why Nomadic Churches frequently hold "open houses" in a home, church office, or other place. To make it easier on guests, Bay Area Community Church spruces up the teachers' lounge of the high school where they meet and holds a monthly "Pizza with the Pastors" social after services.

- Whenever possible, discover why a new attendee does not return to the church. Follow-up calls, visits, and letters with simple evaluation forms can secure these valuable perspectives when visitor contact information has been obtained from guests (such as through a "welcome card" in the Sunday service folder). This gives an opportunity to adjust misperceptions on their part or to make you aware of something that is entirely adjustable on your part.

- Focus on ministries you *can* do to attract and retain visitors— and make them the best they can be. For every event or effort you can't do because of facility complications, you can probably come up with two you can do.

- Be quick to address new obstacles whenever they pose even a slight threat to attracting and assimilating new people. But when facility-related problems *do* arise on a given Sunday morning, feel free to laugh at the bloopers. It's always better to be the one to admit a shortcoming than to give the impression that you didn't even notice.

- Regularly reinforce the truth that your church is the church *now*—not when it has its own building. Leaders combat the "inferiority complex" of some attendees by regularly reminding them of the biblical nature of the church. It quells their questions and stokes the frequency and fervency of their inviting other people to attend. Material in chapter 2 may fuel your thoughts, and we'll say something more about this in the next chapter.

Table 4: Sample Meeting Places for Mobile Churches

Examples of Places Nomadic Churches Meet for Services, Programs, and Events	
• Public and private elementary, middle, and high schools	• Funeral homes
	• Lodges (Elks, VFW, etc.)
• Movie, dinner, and amphitheaters	• Park pavilions
	• Business parks
• Private residential homes	• Barns
• College campuses	• Bars
• Boys and Girls Clubs	• Shopping centers
• Other churches' buildings	• Roller rinks
• Auditoriums	• Factories
• Hotels and motels	• Day-care centers
• Community and recreation centers	• Visitor centers
	• Dance and comedy clubs
• Outdoor tents	• Warehouses
• YMCA / YWCA centers	• Conference and retreat centers

- Sprung structures
- Industrial plants
- Gyms and sports complexes
- Restaurants and banquet halls
- Game and family-fun centers
- City halls
- Firehouse and police stations
- Libraries
- Grange halls
- Bowling alleys
- Yacht clubs
- And just about anywhere else a group can be more or less adequately accommodated at the desired time within the acceptable cost

Responses to Financial Challenges

Although there are more modest figures, the annual operating budgets of several Nomadic Churches we've studied are in the top one percent in the nation. This alone demonstrates that Nomadic Churches can stand on solid financial footing. Yet these churches and other less wealthy ones admit to facing financial stresses, burdens, and complications related to and resulting from their portable status. As we've come to expect, effective nomadic leaders refuse to let these challenges snuff out their mission. Here are some things that have helped them.

- Celebrate the savings. With little exception, Nomadic churches are far less expensive to begin and operate than comparably sized churches in their area. Pete van der Harst, president of Portable Church Industries, goes so far as to say, "The operating cost for a portable church is approximately one third the monthly amount needed for mortgage, maintenance and utilities. The up-front savings are even more impressive, usually on the order of ten to one."[7]

- Keep rental costs in perspective. Even in those rare cases where a Nomadic Church spends as much as or more on its total facilities than a typical church its size (usually just very large churches in developed urban/suburban areas who also rent ministry centers), it's worthwhile to remember that those facilities are actually a big part of what brings the money in to begin with. In other words, were it not for being able to rent places— even expensive ones—that can accommodate a growing church, then the church would have even less overall income. Other advantages of renting rather than owning also help keep facility costs in perspective (see table 2 in chapter 1).

- Shop around for meeting facilities. The price tag can vary drastically. When one church was displaced for a summer from the school they rented, they ended up in a community center. It was just as good as their previous site and saved them $300 a week. "It's been four years and we haven't looked back once," says the pastor. When The Evergreen Community in Portland, Oregon (www.evergreenlife.org) looked for its first meeting facility, they weren't sure if $50 per hour was a reasonable rate to pay for the banquet facilities of a pub. Then they found out the church across the road pays nearly $200 per hour to use the community center. "We may have to go to two services sooner, but even that's not bad," says lead pastor Bob Hyatt. After looking around for a new meeting place, Community Bible Church (www.cbcweb.org) in Vernon, Ohio, settled on a large Grange hall. "It fits our rural community," says pastor Kevin Rees. They pay for maintenance to the building but "at one dollar per year there's so much more we can do now!" he enthusiastically says. For meetings other than corporate worship services, consider parks, other churches' buildings, the (sometimes free) rooms of fire stations, and other economical places. Just don't wait for the "perfect" place; it doesn't exist!

- Put your money where your mission is. Just because you *can* do something, doesn't mean you *should* do it. Fiscally healthy Nomadic Churches selectively choose to invest or not invest their limited money, time, space, and energy according to how well an expense, program, or event reflects or works out the church's priorities.[8]

- Save for a future building according to your philosophy of ministry. One church waited fifteen years before launching a building campaign. Others never plan to build. At the other end of the spectrum, a church launched a major building program when it was two years old, and it has always deposited 12 percent of the weekly offerings for their future campus regardless of what comes in. It all boils down to philosophy. Is your goal to be a regional church with a sprawling campus? Is it to spawn as many new churches as possible? Is it to decentralize onto multiple campuses? Whatever it is, the amount you save for future real estate should reflect it—*after* you've sufficiently funded your current mission. At any stage of a church the meeting facilities should be seen as a support for the mission—not the mission itself.

- Staff the church. The core churches in our study all have multiple-person paid staffs. These people are critical in responding to facility-related challenges and otherwise bolstering the church. Accordingly, their salaries are offset by the net gain their efforts bring. This is also true of facility coordinators, who we're told usually save the church far more than it pays for the salary. At the same time, don't assume by "staffing" that we automatically mean "pay full-time pastors." A commitment to leadership development, lay pastors, strong teams, and internships can allow you to accomplish great things for God and to bring the right person onto the paid staff (full- or part-time) at the right time.

- Buy in bulk. Purchasing large quantities of the supplies you constantly use adds up to impressive savings over time.

- Use any on-site equipment and storage that the host will allow you to have. Every square foot you gain and every piece of equipment you borrow save money. Even if the equipment isn't the best, borrowing it from the host or other churches allows you time to save up the money and spend it on better equipment when you're able and ready.

- Protect your equipment. Use padded and lockable carrying cases for video projection units and stable racks for stacking sound boards. Secure equipment like screens and light stands if they're anywhere near the flow of traffic. Fasten power cords to the floor so that they're not tripped over and equipment doesn't come crashing down. Closed rolling cabinets insulate their contents better than open rolling carts. Traction coverings on ramps leading out of trailers reduce slipping. Covered crates and storage bins prevent most spills. You get the point: The more you protect your present investments, the less future investments you'll have to make.

• Consider the *total* cost. Say you need to bring chairs for your younger children's classes each Sunday because there are none at the rental site. When you price chairs, you find a good deal on seventy-five plastic molded chairs. But before you purchase them, consider other ramifications. You may need to buy more storage or another trailer just to store and transport them each week! It may save you a bundle in the long run to buy slightly more expensive chairs that fold for easier storage, transportation, and setup. Similarly, if a custom van can double for Sunday setup and other transportation uses (e.g., youth group trips), buying two vans may be a better overall investment than purchasing one large truck and trailer.

• Early setup can pay off. Preparing the facility on Saturday evenings for Sunday services (when permissible) typically incurs extra rental costs. That's enough for many churches to dismiss the idea outright. However, early setup may mean more people are free to help and the job can be done quicker and better than doing it all early Sunday. The total rental time, therefore, may actually be less. Plus, there's less rush with equipment (thus, reduced wear and tear), less surprises (thus, time to work through snags), less hassle on Sunday (thus, more time to present quality services), more options for facility workers (thus, easier recruiting), and more time for everyone to focus on guests and other priorities on Sunday (thus, more spiritual and numerical growth).

• Draw on your resident talent. Within your church are an amazing wealth and diversity of experience, gifts, talents, ingenuity, passions, and resources. How do we know that? Not only by studying numerous churches, but because we understand the very nature of the church (e.g., Rom 12; 1 Cor 12; Eph 4). God always provides what a church needs! Your job is to discover and unleash these hidden assets. When Nomadic Churches do so, many find that their systems improve and their costs reduce. We know of churches who tapped into the services of members and saved many thousands of dollars. You can too!

- Check the accounts. Rental costs and contracts can be cumbersome and confusing. Whether by oversight or intention, some churches are unfairly charged more than they owe. A good accountant can catch most discrepancies. Through the vigilance of their bookkeeper, Occoquan Bible Church detected a $21,000 error after being illegitimately charged an obscure fee for two years. The church then enjoyed a few weeks "on the house"!

- Don't pay for what you don't use. Most churches do not use every space or all the equipment in their rental sites. Usually, places like schools have a "room use fee." Make sure whatever you actually use is specified in the contract and updated as soon as changes are made. When the host closes all or part of the facility for things like cleaning or repair, you'll have a contract to fall back on to support a reduction in your fees. It will also help you verify the accuracy of your bills.

- Buy what you need to use. Just because something (e.g., portable freestanding lights) may not be used in your future rental or permanent building doesn't mean you shouldn't buy it—especially if it reflects your values and fulfills your goals. Plus, you never know what you might actually need in the future, and it can always be sold—or given to a new Nomadic Church!

- Cut elective costs whenever possible. If an adequate learning center can be fashioned out of the dead space at the end of a hall, don't rent another room. If putting one class in an unused wing of a school means you'll have to pay for the utilities of that whole wing, look for other options. If you can join another church for a program or project instead of renting another site, at least consider the possibility. If you can lease instead of purchase expensive equipment (especially if you may never need it again in another meeting place), that may save you money in the long run. Many expenses can be shaved down and some outright eliminated with creativity and planning.

- Budget for all ministries. If you can't afford it, don't do it. Don't stifle targeted giving, but encourage people only to give to an individual ministry when they can do so above and beyond their regular giving to the general fund. That way, you won't have one or two robust "pet programs" and nowhere the church can afford to meet!

- Be a good tenant. Facility transitions cost money, whether in time spent finding a place, advertisement of the change, equipment upgrades needed for the new site, and more. So make your payments promptly, if not early. Invest in the facilities in ways that mutually benefit the host and your church. Ask the host how your church can be better guests. Just like a landlord who is pleased with his tenants, a host may be more hesitant to raise rental rates or dismiss those who are considered to be assets to the property. In most cases, it'll cost less to invest in your relationship with the host than to find a new one altogether.

- Encourage biblically based, sacrificial stewardship. Without belaboring the issue, successful Nomadic Churches don't shy away from discussing giving. They teach healthy stewardship from the pulpit, through small groups and class studies, and by offering finance-related seminars. The leaders also model it for their members. After all, giving is commanded, churches need money, and generosity is a mark of maturity.

- Inform your members of your financial status. Although guests don't want to hear detailed financial updates, your regulars need to. People are much more likely to give when they know the needs and where their money will be spent. They may even offer a lower-cost solution. Just remember, people are more apt to give to a dynamic vision that meets needs than to the needs themselves! So again, we suggest you emphasize your vision, even when money matters are discussed.

- Values speak louder than words. If it's essential to *say* what's important, it's even more powerful to *show* it! Soon after Rolling Hills Community Church (www.rollinghills.org) began as a Nomadic Church near Portland, pastor Dale Ebel articulated a simple core value: "Christ first, people second, buildings third." Only now—in their twenty-sixth year of ministry and with over 5,000 people calling them home—are they building a permanent worship center on their campus. Similarly, pastor Ken Hutcherson of Antioch Bible Church (www.abchurch.org) near Seattle says: "Our whole philosophy is people first, programs second, and buildings third."[9] Their twenty-year history in rented facilities, ministering to thousands of people and being involved in planting hundreds of churches, has proven his words to be true.

When leaders guide their congregation with sensitivity, creativity, intentionality, teachability, biblical truth, authentic professionalism, thoughtful prioritizing, strategic planning, a missional mindset, financial prudence, and personal example, the visitor and financial challenges of portability can be endured and overcome. Indeed, they can be demolished! Robust Nomadic Churches will be meeting in a variety of places across the country this Sunday as undeniable proof. That's good news, because no facility situation should ever be allowed to hinder *the* Good News!

Talk Time for Teams

For Pre-Plant Teams

- In addition to what we've offered, what else might you do to prevent or lessen the impact of visitor challenges raised in the previous chapter? Financial challenges?

- What will you do to develop a high quality (but realistic) marketing plan and virtual presence?

- How will your church decentralize into the community—on purpose?

139

- What advantages do you foresee about not owning a traditional church building and operating as a Nomadic Church instead? How will you capitalize upon them?

- Are you committed to remaining people-oriented and showing people that you care, despite all the extra facility-related demands you'll face? How do you plan to do so?

- Based on this book and other church planting resources, develop a master list of site selection criteria to evaluate potential meeting places.

- Develop a mock "quality control checklist" ("excellence inspection") that lists examples of details of the morning routine you'd like to see carried out so that no little touch is missed. What kinds of things appear? Why?

- How do you anticipate connecting with visitors outside of the regular rental period? Soliciting their input if they don't return to your church?

- If you haven't yet, develop a realistic master budget for your first year as a church. Factor in such costs as salaries (including housing, allowances, and insurance), rental facilities, marketing, equipment and supplies, and program expenses. Typically, most of the initial budget is designated toward equipment, marketing, and administration (including staff compensation and facilities). Does your budget match your mission? How do you anticipate meeting your funding goals? Have you gleaned any ideas to shave expenses?

- How does a future campus/building factor into your philosophy of ministry? How and when will it be reflected in your budgeting priorities?

- What will you do to protect your equipment from the rigors of portability?

- If you've reached out to a more experienced Nomadic Church for guidance, see what tactics you can glean from them in dealing with visitor and financial challenges.

- Does your anticipated approach to ministry need to be adjusted in order to carry out the responses offered above? How?

- If you do not have corporate mission, vision, and values statements, spend the time to develop and fashion them into a cohesive philosophy of ministry.[10] Then let that guide you in deciding what to do and what not to do.

For Post-Plant Teams

- Revisit (or develop) your corporate mission, vision, and values statements. Are you really allowing those to guide you in deciding what to do and what not to do? How can you tell? How can you do better?

- Are you taking full advantage of your marketing dollars to make you visible in the community? What can you do to get more "bang for your buck"?

- How can you improve your virtual presence? Is there someone within your congregation who can help? Is it worth paying for a marketing/Web site design consultant?

- How does your church decentralize into the community? How can you do that more intentionally and productively to broaden your influence?

- What advantages have you experienced because you do not own a traditional church building but operate as a Nomadic Church instead? How have you capitalized upon them? How can you do so even more?

- Are you giving your visitors enough personal attention and showing them you care? How can you improve?

- If you had to find a new meeting location next month, what kind of place would you look for? How does your previous and present experience in rented facilities factor in? What are realistic possibilities in your community? If it's been a while since your last facility relocation, it may be time to do some research to see if there is a site in your area that may be more functional and economical for your church. Would Saturday evening setup help?

- From the parking on, how can you make your site more "user-friendly" to guests and regulars? Can you make better external and internal signs—including banners, maps, and diagrams—as well as make better use of them?

- If you don't have one, develop a "quality control checklist" ("excellence inspection") that lists every detail of the morning routine so that no little touch is missed. Is there anything you haven't been doing that could be added? Empower the facility coordinator to help craft and enforce this document.

- How do you connect with visitors outside of the regular rental period? Solicit their input if they don't return to your church? How can you do both better?

- Would your community miss your church if you disappeared tomorrow? Why or why not?

- How does a future campus/building factor into your philosophy of ministry? Are your plans reflected in your budget?

- What are you doing to protect your equipment from the rigors of portability? How can you improve in this area?

- How can your budget more accurately reflect your mission, vision, and values? What changes need to be made for that to happen?

- Can you more intentionally discover and draw upon the resident talent in your church to overcome facility-induced challenges and save money?

- If you've adopted a younger Nomadic Church in your area, share your experience in handling visitor and financial challenges. Are there ways you can share resources?

- In addition to what we've offered, what else have you done to prevent or lessen the impact of visitor challenges like those raised in the previous chapter? Financial challenges?

- Of all the ideas presented above and others you've discussed, which will you actually *implement* to help prevent or alleviate your facility-related visitor and financial challenges? Who will be responsible to do so? What is the timeline for beginning and evaluating these new measures?

CHAPTER TEN

IT'S ALL IN THE ATTITUDE

Attitudes play a far greater role in the success of effective Nomadic Churches than most people realize. By attitude we mean the "combination of presuppositions, beliefs, convictions, and opinions that make up one's habitual stance at any given time toward a subject, person, or act."[1] Because these "mental positions" represent what a person thinks and drive what a person does, we think it's fair to say that having the right attitudes and putting them into action *is* what makes a church successful.

"When I set up a speaker or plug in a monitor, I know that it is connected to a soul somewhere. That person will come and hear the message because we did our part to help set up. I cannot preach or sing, but I can set up, so when someone comes to Christ, we all had a hand in it, and we rejoice together as a team!" —Bennett Gum, Levite at New Hope Christian Fellowship

From the outset, we anticipated testing whether effective nomadic leaders possess a positive attitude. We surmised that such an attitude would be critical to the success of a mobile church in the face of the formidable challenges we've already seen. That proved to be true. Yet in the research process, we actually identified *eight* critical attitudes. We call them "The Eight 'P-Attitudes' of Growing Nomadic Churches" (table 5). While healthy church leaders with their own building may also reflect some or all of these attitudes, we found that these are instrumental in helping growing Nomadic Churches prevent, alleviate, or overcome their facility-related difficulties. Some attitudes find their most poignant expression during the Sunday experience, while others extend to the entire nomadic experience.

Table 5: Attitudinal Responses to Facility-Related Challenges

The Eight "P-Attitudes" of Growing Nomadic Churches			
Positive Attitude	Present-Tense Attitude	Possessive Attitude	Paranoid Attitude
Pliable Attitude	Purpose-Driven Attitude	People-Focused Attitude	Prayerful Attitude

We also found that these attitudes actually *lead* to tactical (action-oriented) responses. In turn, the constructive response frequently results in continued growth and maximized ministry. Finally, the experience of a desirable outcome tends to reinforce the original attitude and perpetuate a healthy cycle (see figure 4).

Figure 4: Relationship Between Response
Attitudes, Actions, and Outcomes

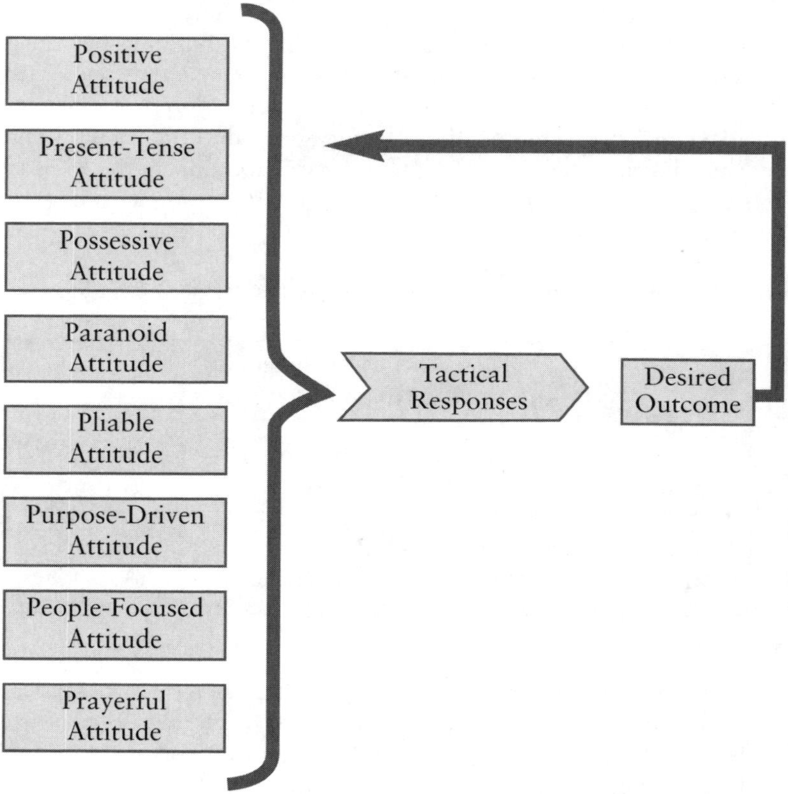

Positive Attitude
Present-Tense Attitude
Possessive Attitude
Paranoid Attitude
Pliable Attitude
Purpose-Driven Attitude
People-Focused Attitude
Prayerful Attitude

Tactical Responses → Desired Outcome

This process doesn't necessarily happen consciously; the matrix of human thinking-acting rarely does. But it *does* happen—sometimes instinctively, sometimes intuitively, and sometimes downright "accidentally." In any case this cycle underlies the experience of effective Nomadic Churches. In the big picture, this makes the attitudes at least as significant as the actions they cause to happen.

The results can be explosive when a whole congregation catches these P-'tudes!

These eight foundational attitudes are presented in a somewhat logical flow rather than by priority or importance. The opening words of each principle—"cultivate, model, and encourage"—are used because we've consistently seen how the attitudes nomadic leaders personally develop, exemplify, and propagate tend to influence similar attitudes in other leaders and members.

Cultivate, Model, and Encourage a Positive Attitude

You get a certain vibe listening to successful nomadic leaders. It's energetic, steady, upbeat. Unlike some floundering portable churches, it pervades the entire organization. It warms you when the church phone is answered, it brightens even the dimmest of meeting places, and it draws you in when you read the church's literature or visit its Web site. It's because of this mysterious force that you won't hear bitter complaints about the meeting site from the pulpit, or hear a worship service start with a defeatist plea for money, or be bombarded with a desperate, manipulative recruitment scheme for more workers. As a visitor, you might actually think church is a great place to be!

The glue that keeps Nomadic Churches together and growing over the rough roads they travel is a shared positive attitude!

Successful nomadic leaders cultivate, model, and influence others with a hopeful, optimistic, and expectant mindset, disposition, and outlook when confronted with facility-related challenges and toward the mobile experience in general. You can not only see it; you can feel it!

On our questionnaire every leader marked "a positive attitude" as a key way they and their church have prevented and responded to their portability challenges. Every survey and interview question designed to test for this attitude confirmed that a highly positive perspective pervades effective Nomadic Churches. Even after we probed the most difficult of facility-related challenges, leaders invariably pointed out multiple advantages of being a Nomadic Church (table 2) and "the bright side" of otherwise problematic issues.[2] People steeped in the negative and dwelling on the frustrations of the portable paradigm wouldn't so quickly and excitedly extol its blessings. The future isn't very bright for those who do otherwise.

An associate of Occoquan Bible Church is grateful for the contagiously optimistic attitude of pastor-teacher Kyle Austin: "He's always able to find the good in a situation." Jeff Carroll of Trinity Community Church advises new nomadic leaders: "Stay positive. If you get negative and lose the vision, your people will too." A paid facility coordinator who is on the frontlines of the weekend battle exclaimed, "Sometimes all you *can* do is be positive!"

Being positive is far from the "last resort," however, as seen in Seneca Creek's slogan: "Absolutely, positively life-changing!" The recording on their senior pastor's voicemail put a smile on our faces each time we heard it. Bruce Johnson's concluding, "Have a grrrrrreat day!" is reminiscent of Kellogg's icon Tony the Tiger—a picture of the positive outlook. Like the other P-Attitudes, Bruce strongly believes that "being positive must emanate from the point person so everyone can catch it." Surely that's why "a positive mental attitude" is listed as a key qualification of their facility coordinator and servants. It's not surprising that it shows up in their service.

"To us being a homeless church is not an impediment. . . . It is only one if you see it as one. See it as an asset, and it will cause you to become more creative and resourceful. It will compel you to develop more people rather than complain about fewer resources."
—Wayne Cordeiro, Pastor, New Hope Christian Fellowship

It's easy to be positive when everything is smooth sailing on calm waters. But as we've seen, that's not the normal conditions for a Nomadic Church. The leaders of effective Nomadic Churches aren't blissfully ignorant about their facility-related challenges nor naive about the negative impact unaddressed challenges can have. They freely share that homelessness is hard. But the maintenance of a positive attitude *amid* rather than in the absence of pressing challenges is even greater confirmation of the importance of this attitude in the life of a mobile ministry.

Cultivate, Model, and Encourage a Present-Tense Attitude

Another prominent attitudinal response to challenges inherent in the mobile model is maintaining a "present-tense attitude." By this we essentially mean living in and maximizing the present, rather than obsessing about the future or something the church does not yet have. We found two related convictions that permeate the mindset of grounded nomadic leaders.

We Are the Church Now

The first theme involves the essence of the Nomadic Church. Successful Nomadic Churches are well aware that they *presently* are part of Christ's *ekklesia* and ontologically equal to any other Christian church. They embrace their legitimacy as an expression of the universal church and that this cherished spiritual status is not contingent upon where they meet, in what kind of place they assemble, or how frequently they relocate. They know they are the church—the most holy place of God's dwelling—whether meeting in a cathedral or a cafeteria.[3]

On the questionnaires we distributed, every respondent indicated that a thoroughly biblical grasp of their church's true identity is a key way they prevent and respond to certain facility-related challenges.

This conviction is primarily communicated through the content of teaching and the disposition of leading. Leaders confidently assert that they instruct their congregation about what does and doesn't make a church a true church. This may be anything from a theme in an entire message series to a brief reminder at the conclusion of an annual report. Such matters are regularly addressed in orientation (membership) courses and even in the ecclesiology section of doctrinal statements.

When you continually reinforce that your congregation is *presently* the church, your people can function *as* the church.

Regular instruction of this type has many benefits. It alleviates ugly envy of other churches' facilities, lessens anxiety about lacking a permanent facility, stimulates members to invite more people, and, as Seneca Creek Community Church's ministry philosophy ends, it leads to "not selfishly clinging to the people and resources God has entrusted to us." It's precisely because of this biblical emphasis that the congregants of bustling Nomadic Churches seldom have an "inferiority complex" (see chapter 8).

We Minister as the Church Now

The second closely related aspect of a present-tense attitude concerns the ministry of the Nomadic Church. Part of our questionnaires were designed to ascertain if the participant has a definite sense of immediacy about ministry, which we clarified as having an insatiable compulsion not to wait to "do ministry" until a building is secured. All of our respondents who identified themselves as embracing this outlook and believe that it contributes to their success. As one leader told us: "Our facilities may be temporary, but our ministry sure isn't!"

Like the other P-attitudes, this one leads to action. A casual perusal of the literature of growing Nomadic Churches authenticates that they are not content to wait passively to minister until they have their own building, an "ideal" meeting place, or any other future convenience. There is a clear sense of urgency to minister aggressively now. One pastor even shared that his leaders had done such a good job of permeating the church with this mindset that when it actually came time to launch a building campaign, it took an enormous amount of energy just to get people on board! He also recognizes how this attitude, like the others, will serve them well when they finally do build on the land they currently own.

Vibrant Nomadic Churches refuse to wait until a building is constructed or a better facility is secured before they roll up their sleeves and enthusiastically serve the Lord and people. That's the only way to make a lasting difference while in temporary facilities.

Cultivate, Model, and Encourage a Possessive Attitude

When a Nomadic Church has a robust present-tense attitude, it is released to have a "possessive attitude" toward its rental facilities. Generally speaking, to possess or be possessive is to have a sense of belonging, ownership, or territorial dominion, or to occupy or seize a place regardless of whether the occupants have legal ownership rights. In a constructive sense, this characterizes the manner in which skilled Nomadic Churches mentally view their rental facilities.

Working with the host and within their guidelines, nomadic pastors do whatever is necessary to make the leased facilities their own while they are there. They embed a sense of ownership and stewardship among their leaders. The movie theater or school building is *their* church building for the day; it "belongs" to them. They care for it as if it were their own. The temporary "ownership rights" purchased by their rent invigorates a healthy sense of "territorial dominion" that leads them, in the words of one facility servant, to "possess and transform" the site to be as conducive as possible to achieving ministry objectives. Another leader explained during a visit we made: "We put our stamp on this place however we can."

151

Taking possession of a facility and treating it as if it were yours is a definite plus in the portable paradigm!

A possessive attitude shines most clearly in the many detailed modifications and enhancements made to the meeting site during the rental period. And it's not just sloppy decorations. A core value of many of the churches we've studied goes something like this: "Excellence matters because it honors God and inspires people." We doubt that many touches of excellence would be made if the churches timidly or lazily occupied their building. Instead, this attitude and the resultant actions are a substantial part of what separates flourishing Nomadic Churches from floundering ones.

Cultivate, Model, and Encourage a Paranoid Attitude

A complement to a possessive attitude is a "paranoid attitude." According to the dictionary, "paranoia" can be viewed as "excessive mental distrust, often linked with a mission." One nomadic leader attributed his concept of a paranoid attitude to Andy Grove, Intel's successful former CEO, who is fond of saying "only the paranoid survive"! This mindset helped Intel take over a greater share of the market in the years Grove was at the helm, and it's helping Nomadic Churches everywhere take greater spiritual ground with each passing year.

A church's "mission" is too critical to leave to chance, too vital to "trust" it will advance unhindered. Sunday services and other ministries are too important to assume that they will go on in temporary facilities without many challenges and surprises. Not only do the paranoid survive—they thrive!

Make sure that "Murphy" isn't in the room when your worship begins!

This paranoid attitude leads to a mindset of rigorous preparedness, decisive responsiveness, and insightful anticipation of various challenges. Leaders take concrete steps to preempt disaster. Sometimes by intention and sometimes just instinctively, tools like detailed quality-control checklists prevail. One senior pastor commented, "We have created a culture where we're paranoid . . . that something could break or go wrong, that we could miss something. We have backups and 'plan Bs' for everything." A positive outlook needs to be balanced with an "excessive mental distrust" that all will be perpetually well. As one leader advises, "It's not a given that Sunday will happen. Things *will* go wrong, and you have to be ready."

Cultivate, Model, and Encourage a Pliable Attitude

The two previous attitudes are appropriately balanced by an equally compelling mindset of pliability. To be "pliable" is to be "flexible, supple, adjusting readily, and adaptable." Similarly, to be "flexible" is to be "capable of being bent, without breaking." A word you inevitably hear when talking to nomadic leaders is "flexibility."[4] It's a "do or die" mindset for mobile ministries.

"Flexibility is necessary to survive," especially since "no Sunday is ever really 'typical'!"—A Facilities Coordinator

Pliable people are comfortable with modification or adaptation. One pastor advises that a new church planter "develop a clear plan with flexibility built within it," while another church's Philosophy of Organization says, "Organization needs to be both flexible and simple for the greatest growth to occur." It takes a flexible mindset to produce a flexible organization, and it takes a flexible church to produce a flourishing ministry, especially in a portable setting. An inflexible disposition invites disastrous consequences, while a pliable outlook helps a church readily adapt and adjust when encountering persistent and spontaneous demands and challenges. That's certainly why the seasoned leaders we studied gave themselves high marks on their flexibility, and it's why we could personally see many examples of it in action on our visits to their churches. We feel quite comfortable saying that without flexibility, mobile ministries *will* break!

Cultivate, Model, and Encourage a Purpose-Driven Attitude

A sixth attitude that has proven beneficial in preventing and working through facility-related challenges is a "purpose-driven attitude."[5] Because of the many distractions that assail churches who use rented facilities, prudent leaders instinctively and intentionally focus on the "why" of everything they attempt. They not only develop compelling corporate statements (mission, vision, values, etc.), they also advertise and reinforce them in every conceivable way in order to saturate their congregation's mindset with their purposes. They measure their goals and outcomes by them, and they frequently appeal to them as justification for how they interpret and respond to their challenges. They allow nothing to stand in the way of transforming these written statements of what *should* be into real stories that *are!*

Purposeful perspective leads to purposeful action, including strategic steps to continue growing, fulfill the church's mission, and meet ministry objectives even in the face of daunting homeless hardships.

Although this attitude doesn't usually *remove* facility-related obstacles, it compels urgent, efficient, and persevering responses to them. When a ministry is tough to offer, a purpose-filled church will find a solution and gladly do it anyway, because they have resolved not to let anything impede their priorities.

Cultivate, Model, and Encourage a People-Focused Attitude

The terms "portable" and "people" should never be mutually exclusive in a Christian church. One would think that the absence of a building would translate into more focus on people. Not always so. One of the things often heard in the third or fourth year of a typical church plant is, "Pastor, when are we going to become a *real* church?" The "real" refers to the church owning their own building. To counter this, effective nomadic leaders continually remind their congregation that the priority is making an impact on people's lives with the gospel.

While some of the other attitudes are more intuitive, transformational Nomadic Churches very intentionally cultivate, emphasize, and communicate a conviction that *people* are the priority. When we pushed interviewees on the fundamental assumption behind certain things their church does, the responses inevitably boiled down to a statement made by more than one participant, "The glory of God and the good of his people." This ministry focal point is reflected in the churches' teaching, corporate statements, programs, staffing, budget, and literature. And, yes, it shows in the lives of the congregation, too!

The mindset that "people matter" puts facilities and their attendant challenges in perspective. It also motivates efficient, creative, and resourceful responses to those challenges. Meeting facilities may be important to portable churches, but the reason is that they are *tools* to help strengthen believers and reach unbelievers.[6]

Like the other attitudes, a people-focused attitude is valuable for all churches. However, since this attitude motivates strategic responses to many present and potential facility-related challenges, nomadic leaders should let it envelop their own thinking and the mindset of the entire congregation. People are too important in God's economy for anything less!

Cultivate, Model, and Encourage a Prayerful Attitude

Like other attitudes, prayer is typically thought of in terms of action (actual communication with God) but is, in reality, preceded and governed by an attitude—certain presuppositions, convictions, and beliefs. Like all but one of the other attitudes, we did not intentionally set out to discern whether a prayerful attitude pervades successful Nomadic Churches. We were impressed to discover how much it actually does.

Godly nomadic leaders don't just talk about prayer, they pray. Without our prompting, leaders usually volunteered to open or close our interviews in prayer. On our visits we saw—and were even invited to join in—the morning prayer times of facility crews and worship teams. Prayer groups, calendars, request lists, vigils, meetings, e-groups, and specially designated prayer areas are considered by leaders to be integral to the life of their eternally minded churches.

"There is much we can do after we pray; but there's nothing worth doing until we pray." —Core Value of Seneca Creek Community Church

The explanation of Trinity Community Church's vision calls members to "regular times of personal prayer and frequently [to] pray both corporately and privately, joining in the public prayers for unity in the Spirit and spending moments of silence in thanksgiving, confession and petition before God." Pastor Jeff Carroll advises new nomadic leaders, "Pray hard!" The very first of Seneca Creek Community Church's "Ten Keys to Building a Truly Great Church" is "a powerful and pervasive prayer ministry that regularly believes God for the impossible." Bay Area Community Church is looking forward to a prayer room in their new facility as yet another way to fulfill their core value: "Faithful Prayer—depending continually on our Lord for wisdom and provision." The first time we contacted New Life Christian Church and introduced the subject of this research, senior pastor Brett Andrews commented, "One thing I can tell you; we pray a lot."[7]

Nomadic leaders will want to ensure that they and all their church does are immersed in this attitude and the action to which it leads—prayer itself. We will never know exactly how much this prayerful attitude contributes to the success of growing Nomadic Churches.[8] But we're confident that a presupposition of the importance of prayer and the resulting act of consistent prayer open up the infinite resources of Almighty God (e.g., Matt 7:7-11; Eph 6:18-20; Jas 5:16-18). Surely, that is among the wisest possible attitudinal and tactical responses to any challenge, facility-related or not!

Conclusion

Although other attitudes may be integral to vibrant Nomadic Churches, these eight surfaced as dominant and vital. Facilities aside for a moment, we believe these attitudes are essential to the success of *any* Christian church. But these mindsets specifically help Nomadic Churches prevent and otherwise counter their facility-related challenges. Most—if not all—of the tactical responses in the previous chapters flow out of one or more of these attitudes in some manner (see figure 4). Perhaps now you can see why we enthusiastically say, "It's all in the attitude!"

Talk Time for Teams

For Pre-Plant Teams

- How important have you considered "attitude" to be in the success of a church? Has this chapter shaped your thinking toward attitudes? How?

- Go back and write in your own words a definition of each attitude based on the information we've given, a dictionary, and your own insights. What biblical support can you add for each?

- Do you agree that these eight attitudes are—or should be—integral to your Nomadic Church? Why or why not?

- What in your lives, ministry, and training up to this point has prepared you to "own" each of these attitudes?

- Of the eight attitudes, which ones do you most need to work on cultivating? Which ones come most naturally? Evaluating your team as a whole, are there any glaring attitudinal blind spots?

- How important do you consider the attitudes of leadership to be in shaping the mindset of a congregation? How might you go about doing so?

- Do your own convictions or anticipated approach to ministry need to be adjusted in order to incorporate the suggested attitudes? How?

- If you've reached out for guidance to a more experienced Nomadic Church in your denomination or geographical area, spend some time discussing how the eight P-attitudes have an impact on their ministry in both philosophical and practical ways. Be open to other attitudes they might suggest that have been critical to their success.

- Take some time to pray for the Lord to help you generate a greater appreciation and application of each of the eight attitudes in this chapter.

For Post-Plant Teams

- How important do you consider "attitude" to be to the success of a church? Why?

- Go back and write in your own words a definition of each attitude based on the information we've given, a dictionary, and your own insights. What biblical support can you add for each?

- Do you agree that these eight attitudes are—or should be—integral to your church? Why or why not?

- Examine each attitude carefully. Rate yourself individually and then your church corporately on a scale of 1 to 10, with "1" indicating a clear void of the attitude and "10" signifying a deep understanding and consistent reflection of the attitude. Afterward,
  (a) Share your scores and *why* you gave the marks you did.
  (b) Discuss how you've seen each emphasis at work in your lives and the mindset of your church.
  (c) Is there any cause for conviction? For celebration?
  (d) How have possessing and passing on these attitudes helped you personally? As a church?
  (e) Where could you use "an attitude adjustment"? What are some ways you can make any necessary changes?

- Can you think of any instances where your commitment to these attitudes has been challenged? How well did you respond? How could you have responded even better?

- How important do you consider the attitudes of leadership to be in shaping the mindset of your congregation? How have you gone about doing so? How might you improve?

- Have you seen figure 4 work out in your experience? How?

- If you've adopted a newer Nomadic Church in your denomination or geographical area, share your experience about how these eight attitudes (and, if any, others) have had an impact on your ministry. Give concrete examples and encouragement.

- Take some time to pray for the Lord to help you generate a greater appreciation and application of each of the eight attitudes in this chapter.

Conclusion

WHAT'S A NOMADIC CHURCH TO DO?

Like rugged nomads, we've traveled a lot of ground in a short time. It's time to end our trek together and launch you on the rest of yours. If you've participated in the "Talk Times," you've probably already extended our work. So in order not to be redundant, we'll leave you with just three broad exhortations that capture much of the essence of this book.

Expect Many Challenges

Three chapters have brought to light a host of facility-related challenges. Although we hope it's not your final impression, one thing our extensive study forcefully confirms is that Nomadic Churches should *expect* to encounter numerous facility-related challenges. It is the normal course of experience. It's realistic, not defeatist. A lack of such "mental readiness" will result in less effective solutions, because responses are more productive when a problem or its possibility is anticipated or recognized. That is partly why growing Nomadic Churches are on such a high state of preparedness each Sunday. As we've seen, however, Sunday is not all that is affected. Challenges across the ministry spectrum must be anticipated, because there are far more potentially problematic areas than initially meet the eye.

It's essential to have a realistic grasp of the current and potential threats in order to fend them off.

One senior pastor advises a new nomadic pastor, "Prepare people in the clearest possible language that this will be hard." Another pastor adds, "Don't underestimate the work. It's an around-the-clock commitment." There is nothing noble about downplaying the dilemmas. As any competent health specialist realizes, diagnosis of the problem precedes prescription for the cure.

To jog your memory, the following table presents select themes of challenges that most Nomadic Churches will perpetually or periodically face. Don't get stuck here, but use this as an awareness tool.

Table 6: Thematic Sample of Facility-Related Challenges

Storage Scarcities	Rent Raises	Legal Liabilities	Training Troubles	Directional Disorder
Climate Concerns	Transportation Trials	Artificial Accusations	Aroma Atrocities	Security Scares
Setup/Breakdown Toil	Display Difficulties	Shadowy Sanctuaries	Privacy Penury	Host-Tenant Tensions
Aesthetic Aggravations	Parking Paucities	Inferiority Idiosyncrasies	Alarming Acoustics	Equipment Exasperations
Pessimistic Perceptions	Facility Finding	Customization Constraints	Extra Expenses	Atmospheric Annoyances
Recruiting Resistance	Event Encumbrances	Practice Problems	Space Shortages	Baptism Blues
Program Pitfalls	Furnishing Faults	Decoration Dilemmas	Staffing Setbacks	Construction Complications

Respond Swiftly and Decisively to Challenges

While three earlier chapters introduced facility-related challenges common to Nomadic Churches, four chapters presented ways to respond to them. It's one thing to anticipate facility-related challenges and quite another to act quickly and decisively to prevent and counter them. Effective Nomadic Churches *pounce* on the challenges. The term "aggressive" isn't an overstatement. Whether it's scraping gum off a movie theater seat that a guest may sit in or strategizing a way to accomplish a critical program, nothing is left to chance. As Martin Luther is credited with saying, "Pray as if everything depends on God. Then work as if everything depends on you." What sage advice for nomadic leaders!

It's been our experience that too many Nomadic Churches play the ostrich game and hope the challenges "just go away." Others seem to relish sitting on the "poor me pity pot," feeling woefully inadequate to meet the challenges. But even when interviewees at flourishing churches asked us what *we* thought they could enhance, our suggestions were often met with a recital of previous or ongoing efforts to remedy the issues we raised. They could only do that because they had cultivated a mindset of attacking challenges. They understand that passivity is poison. With so much to do and so many strains in an upstart church, it would be easy to neglect addressing certain issues. Nevertheless, effective churches do not sit idly by as challenges mount. They take action!

Enjoy the Nomadic Adventure

Exploration is invigorating—at least it *should* be. Sure there are times of exhaustion, moments of indirection, and flashes of frustration. Grumbles, mumbles, and jumbles are part and parcel of portability. But isn't it splendid to be able to grow *through* those seasons with the One who promised, "Surely I am with you always, to the very end of the age" (Matt 28:20*b*)? Isn't it empowering to realize that Christ himself said, "I will build *my* church, and the gates of Hades will not overcome it" (Matt

16:18*b*)? Isn't it energizing to blast through a barrier or plan around a problem "with the power of the Most High," for whom "nothing is impossible" (Luke 1:35, 37)? Our hearts beat faster just thinking about it!

If some part of your soul resonates with what we've said, there's a high likelihood that your heart beats in rhythm with other happily homeless churches and that you have or will lead your nomadic flock to strike spiritual gold in your own purposeful wanderings through this world. As strange as it may sound to the uninitiated, effective nomadic leaders overwhelmingly report that they actually *enjoy* the nomadic adventure!

Thoughtful leaders treasure their portable ministry and maintain a balanced sense of wonder, intensity, and humor about it all. As one lead pastor remarked, "We laugh a lot. . . . People can tell that we actually enjoy our ministry." Perhaps another pastor best summarized this when we asked if he would do it all over again: "It'd be like not having your children. It's got to be the greatest ride in ministry!"

Simply savoring the total package—the challenges, the growth, the opportunities, the disappointments—is a strategy that spurs further tactical action, keeps difficulties in perspective, and bolsters the vigor of a Nomadic Church and the stamina of its leaders. After all, "there is nothing better for a man than to enjoy his work" (Eccl 3:22; cf. 5:18; 8:15). Table 2 in chapter 1 suggests many reasons someone can find meaningful satisfaction leading a Nomadic Church. And why not? Christians are to "put their hope in God, who richly provides us with everything for our enjoyment" (1 Tim 6:17*b*).

We are confident that Nomadic Churches *will continue* to grow spiritually, qualitatively, numerically, and financially.

There was a day when people frowned upon the few, brave churches who remained in rented facilities for multiple years. "Who will want to visit? Who would stay? They can't grow. What a hassle. People won't make serious investments. What's wrong with their priorities? Shouldn't God's people have better?

163

Don't worry, their rolls and books will dry up and the church will blow away soon enough," many skeptics reasoned. Standing on the shoulders of countless examples to the contrary, we are confident that Nomadic Churches *will continue* to grow spiritually, qualitatively, numerically, and financially. In fact, many do so in ways that rival and excel even the best of their sister stationary churches.

What remains for you, our nomadic friends, is to face the challenges inherent in your ministry context and forge a way through or around them. We have offered many thoughts to help you—ideas born out of the struggles and joys of your fellow nomadic congregations. It's your turn to implement and add to our work. There is truth to be told, a world to win, a commission to be championed, work to be worked, character to be crafted, regions to be revived, a good fight to fight, and a Lover to be loved. No matter where your church assembles in ten weeks or in ten years, will you lead your flock to rise to this inspiring, monumental occasion? You're not alone. You can do it. You *must!*

Talk Time for Teams

For Pre-Plant Teams

- Frankly share your level of mental preparedness for the challenges you will soon face.

- How do you plan to encourage one another and your congregation when confronted with challenges inherent in the portable paradigm?

- How might you, your team, and your church grow stronger through facing and responding to challenges?

- Discuss the biblical references and their contexts that are cited in this chapter. How do these shape your perspective on mobile ministry?

- Will you accept the challenge in the closing words of this chapter?

For Post-Plant Teams

- How prepared have you been for the challenges you've faced as a Nomadic Church? Can you be better prepared for future obstacles?

- How have you encouraged one another and your congregation when confronted with portability challenges? How might you do that more or better?

- How have you and your church grown stronger through facing and responding to challenges?

- Can you honestly say that you "enjoy" nomadic life? When is your contentment highest and lowest? How can you increase your satisfaction?

- Discuss the biblical references and their contexts that are cited in this chapter. How do these shape your perspective on mobile ministry?

- Will you accept the challenge in the closing words of this chapter?

You're welcome to e-mail us your responses to any of the "Talk Time" questions at Easum@easumbandy.com.

APPENDIX A

RESOURCE RECOMMENDATIONS

Christian thinkers and ministry practitioners produced an impressive amount of resources during the last half of the twentieth century—a trend that, if anything, has only intensified today. With little exception, however, nothing has addressed the multifaceted challenges, needs, responses, advantages, import, or overall ministry of Nomadic Churches.

For example, contemporary church growth, health, and renewal writers have increasingly noted just how much impact facilities can have on the vitality, development, and expansion of a church. But when discussing a church's facilities, they invariably assume the congregation owns its building(s) and can, more or less, manipulate it at will to trigger the desired effect. Even church planting and management resources rarely discuss the specific issues of unique import to Nomadic Churches. When they do, the focus is almost exclusively on locating, financing, or enhancing facilities to the exclusion of anticipating or handling the stresses that inevitably arise for a church that operates from temporary sites.[1]

With that in mind, we offer several resources below. This list is suggestive, not exhaustive. To save you time and money, Internet links are provided whenever possible. While the inclusion of a work doesn't mean we endorse every part of it, our research and experience have shown that each has at least some excellent content that addresses or can be applied to overcoming challenges faced by Nomadic Churches. Some may surprise you, and some you may already have on your shelf!

Bandy, Thomas, ed. *Net Results: New Ideas in Church Vitality.* Lubbock, Tex. www.netresults.org. Although any church could benefit from the content in this monthly journal, of special interest to Nomadic Churches is the packet of past articles entitled "Church Facilities: Evaluation and Improvement." While the compiled articles don't directly address ministry in a temporary setting, they raise many helpful issues.

Bandy, Thomas. *Road Runner: The Body in Motion.* Nashville: Abingdon Press, 2002. The reader is introduced to the church in motion rather than the church in residence.

Banks, Robert and Julia. *The Church Comes Home.* Peabody, Mass.: Hendrickson, 1998. Although many Nomadic Churches plan eventually to build or acquire permanent worship facilities, in the interim they can learn a lot from those whose philosophy of ministry intentionally keeps them from owning a building. One such example is the house church movement, which is represented well in this visionary yet practical volume by two of its leading proponents.

Baptist General Convention of Texas. *Using a Portable Church.* 1996–1999. www.bgct.org/csc/Portable.html. This brief brochure gives some encouragement and practical pointers on relevant issues.

Barna, George. *The Power of Team Leadership: Achieving Success through Shared Responsibility.* Colorado Springs: Waterbrook, 2001. Maybe even more than static churches, teams make Nomadic Churches go! Accordingly, this comprehensive look at team ministry is a worthwhile read.

Barna, George. Barna Research Group, Ltd. www.barna.org. Since 1984, Barna's full-service marketing research company has provided information and analysis to help church leaders make strategic decisions. Although none have yet to focus specifically on the Nomadic Church, the free monthly reports periodically illuminate aspects of particular interest to Nomadic Churches. Back issues can be searched.

Berkley, James D., ed. *Leadership Handbook of Management and Administration: Practical Insights from a Cross Section of Ministry Leaders.* Grand Rapids: Baker, 1994. At 524 pages, this is apparently the largest Christian text of its kind to date. Although no material is customized to mobile churches, its standard management issues are helpful (e.g., "Volunteer-Staff Supervision," "Managing the Church Office," and "Finances"). More specifically, the thirty-six pages devoted to facility issues give principles that Nomadic Churches can apply with some creativity.

Bowman, Ray. *When* Not *to Build: An Architect's Unconventional Wisdom for the Growing Church.* Rev. and exp. Grand Rapids: Baker, 2000. This stimulating book furnishes a balanced perspective on buildings and a sense of immediacy about ministry. It has applicable advice for how to maximize current meeting space and how to plan for optimal facilities if and when the time to build does come. The self-tests are a definite bonus. Its companion volume, *When* Not *to Borrow: Unconventional Financial Wisdom to Set Your Church Free* (Grand Rapids: Baker, 1996), is more narrowly focused but nearly as valuable.

Callahan, Kennon L. *Twelve Keys to an Effective Church: Strategic Planning for Mission.* San Francisco: Jossey-Bass Publications, 1983. Although this is the oldest book on the list, it raises several issues that Nomadic Churches can either immediately implement or consider when relocating to a new meeting site. Four of the twelve "keys" relate to a church's facility situation. Most issues raised here are surfaced in similar works, but this one offers some helpful strategies for overcoming the facility-induced shortcomings it highlights.

Cordeiro, Wayne. *Doing Church as a Team.* Ventura, Calif.: Regal, 2001. Cordeiro's church, New Hope Community, is mentioned throughout this book. His helpful work on team ministry was born out of the mobile experience.

Cousins, Don, Leith Anderson, and Arthur DeKruyter. *Mastering Church Management.* Mastering Ministry Series. Portland, Ore.: Multnomah, 1990. Though slimmer than Berkley's volume (see above) and also without Nomadic Churches in view, there is some valuable management material. Its early sections provide a rationale for nomadic positions like a facility coordinator. Chapter 3 is a timely reminder about "Staying People Centered and Purpose Driven," while the chapters on "Working through Leaders" and "Motivating and Recruiting

Volunteers" are helpful because of the extra workers Nomadic Churches need.

Donahue, Bill. *The Willow Creek Guide to Leading Life-Changing Small Groups.* Grand Rapids: Zondervan, 1996. This shines as one of the most simple yet usable resources for making any church into a church of small groups that work. Since a common denominator in successful Nomadic Churches is a vital small group ministry, few will want to pass on this book.

Eason, Tim. "Salisbury Church—Charleston, Illinois: A Church on the Go!" *Church Media,* March 2001. www.churchmedia.net/CMU/articles/mediaministry/011.htm. Although it's easy to become outdated in our fast-moving electronic world, this short piece tells what one successful Nomadic Church uses by way of media. For greater media specificity, see Essentric Audio and Video Productions, "Portable Church," www.essentricaudio.com/portachurch.htm.

Easum, Bill. *Team Based Ministry.* EBA Press, 2003. This workbook is a combination of both Bill Easum and Tom Bandy's thoughts on team ministry. You can find it at the Web site www.easumbandy.com in the store under "Workbooks."

Easum, Bill, and Dave Travis. *Beyond the Box: Innovative Churches That Work.* Loveland, Colo.: Group, 2003. From the concluding words of the introduction, Nomadic Churches know they're about to get some focus: "And it's well past time to think beyond one church, beyond existing in a 'sacred' location . . ." Among other nourishment, the overview of decentralized models of ministry (e.g., multisite churches) is worth digesting.

Easum, Bandy, and Associates. "Renting Space." www.easumbandy.com/FAQS/renting_space.htm. As part of the more than 2,000 pages of free resources on this site, this link will take you to some other Nomadic Churches and, more important, their field-tested advice about doing church in rented facilities.

Edwards, Paul and Sarah. *Working from Home: Everything You Need to Know About Living and Working Under the Same Roof.* 5th ed. Los Angeles: J. P. Tarcher, 1999. Although large sections are irrelevant, at 664 pages these home office gurus provide plenty of useful topics for nomadic staff without benefit of a centralized office. Even the home business sections provide some surprising insights. It's tightly integrated with Internet resources, includes checklists and worksheets, and reads like a friendly office manager who loves giving advice to people who work largely out of their home.

Ferguson, Everett. *The Church of Christ: A Biblical Ecclesiology for Today.* Grand Rapids: Eerdmans, 1996. Perhaps even more than other popular ecclesiology texts, this one does an excellent job of grounding a Nomadic Church in its biblical identity as a meaningful, fully legitimate expression of the Church of Christ. As with any theologically oriented work, there is something for everyone to disagree with. Still, many leaders will find the discussions of the images, purposes, worship, assembly, ministry, leadership, and functions of the church to be thoughtful and illuminating.

Fisher, Kimball, and Mareen Duncan. *A Hands On Guide to Managing Off-Site Employees and Virtual Teams.* New York: McGraw-Hill Trade, 2000. Leaders of staff without a centralized meeting place or who utilize multiple campuses can find helpful nuggets in this business book. It covers how to manage off-site employees and virtual teams, including how to communicate with and inspire employees, coach for peak performance, and build a cohesive team comprised of workers in different locations.

George, Carl F. *The Coming Church Revolution: Empowering Leaders for the Future.* Grand Rapids: Fleming H. Revell, 1994. With its relational meta-model emphasis, this work supplies fuel and formulas to Nomadic Churches who yearn to focus on mission and ministry instead of brick and mortar. See George's *Prepare Your Church for the Future* (Grand Rapids: Revell, 1992) for more foundational material on this model that is popular in some form among many Nomadic Churches.

Hanna, Jeff. *Safe and Secure: The Alban Guide to Protecting Your Congregation.* N.p.: Alban Institute, 1999. Nomadic Churches have their fair share of unique security risks. Although portable churches are not in focus, they should pay particular attention to the chapters on building safety and visitor protection so that they can identify threats and develop preventive strategies.

Hesselgrave, David J. *Planting Churches Cross-Culturally: North America and Beyond.* 2d ed. Grand Rapids: Baker, 2000. This popular work for upstart congregations has something to offer even more experienced Nomadic Churches. Although short on addressing the actual challenges of mobile ministries, chapter 8 on "The Believers Congregated" offers very relevant material.

Holcomb, Tim J. *Church Administration from A to Z: Support for Church Growth.* Nashville: Convention Press, 1994. There is little fluff in this handbook for handling church administration. The chapters on information, office, and especially image management (complete with an "Image Audit") are particularly useful.

The Leadership Network. www.leadnet.org. Search with key words like "facilities" and "campus" to yield useful bits from four publications associated with this equipping and lay mobilization network of mostly emergent churches.

Lewis, Brad. "The Portable Church." *Vital Ministry* (March/April 1999). www.onlinerev.com/article.asp?ID=109. This short work rivals all others for its direct benefit. Practical, biblically grounded, and based on interviews with real nomadic leaders, it begins by posing several relevant questions and organizes the responses into eight "Be . . ." principles that Nomadic Churches will want to heed. (While you're at this site, skip over for a quick read of the article "Rx for the Invisible Church," www.onlinerev.com/article.asp?ID=14 and the article "Ways to Make Your Facility Practical," www.onlinerev.com/article.asp?ID=209.)

Longman III, Tremper. *Immanuel in Our Place: Seeing Christ in Israel's Worship.* The Gospel According to the Old Testament. Phillipsburg, N.J.: Presbyterian and Reformed, 2001. Those seeking a more refined understanding of the role and meaning of "sacred space" in Scripture will benefit especially from part one (pp. 1-74) of this accessible volume by a noted scholar.

Maag, Chris. "Church without a Home: Antioch Bible Church Has More Than 3,000 Members, but It Doesn't Have a Building of Its Own." *EastSide Journal,* 5 December 1999. www.eastsidejournal.com/sited/retr_story.pl/ 7156. Here's one of many refreshing examples of the secular media paying

attention to Nomadic Churches. In fact, by comparison main-
stream media outlets seem to have written more on Nomadic
churches than Christians have! Visit Antioch at
www.abchurch.org.

Macchia, Stephen. *Becoming a Healthy Church: 10
Characteristics*. Grand Rapids: Baker, 1999. While all of the
suggested characteristics can nourish Nomadic Churches, two
that deserve special attention in light of the portability plight
are: "The healthy church utilizes appropriate facilities, equipment, and systems to provide maximum support for the
growth and development of its ministries" and "networking
with the Body of Christ." Ken Hemphill tackles some over-
lapping issues in *The Antioch Effect: 8 Characteristics of
Highly Effective Churches* (Nashville: Broadman & Holman,
1994).

McLain, David. "Sacred Sound: Making It Mobile." *Live Sound
International* (January/February 2002), www.livesoundint.com/
archives/2002/janfeb/portable/portable.php. After a real life
example, McLain gives eight characteristics of sound systems
for Nomadic Churches.

McLaren, Brian D. *The Church on the Other Side*. Grand
Rapids: Zondervan, 2003. Of all of McLaren's works, this
may be the most helpful for learning to survive and thrive as a
Nomadic Church in postmodernity. Especially see the call to
"abandon structures as they are outgrown" and to "emphasize
and de-emphasize place."

Malphurs, Aubrey. *Planting Growing Churches for the 21st
Century: A Comprehensive Guide for New Churches and
Those Desiring Renewal*. 2nd ed. Grand Rapids: Baker, 1998.
This is one of the more worthwhile church planting books
available—even for more established Nomadic Churches. In
addition to its other utilities, some parts deal directly with the
Nomadic Church's facility-related issues (e.g., pp. 290-91,
322-33). Assets include criteria for meeting site selection, how
certain sites affect both church attendees and the unchurched
community, and advantages and disadvantages of different
kinds of meeting sites.

Miller, Herb. *How to Build a Magnetic Church*. Creative
Leadership Series, ed. Lyle E. Schaller. Nashville: Abingdon

Press, 1987. Without buildings to draw people, Nomadic Churches must employ other "magnets." Just about each of the nine chapters has something of value when contextualized to Nomadic Churches. The date of the book is seldom annoying to the reader.

Mobile Church Solutions (Passion for Planting). New Life Christian Church in Virginia started this ministry to help Nomadic Churches like themselves. It is part of an overall strategy for church plants that also includes nonprofit organizations for portable equipment (www.church-equipment.com), project management (www.church-planting.net), and marketing (www.church-marketing.com). The overarching organization is Passion for Planting (www.church-planting.net). For free tools, see www.church-marketing.com/church-planting.htm.

Murray, Stuart. *Church Planting: Laying Foundations.* Carlisle, U.K.: Paternoster, 1998. Although more philosophical than practical, many will find its eighth chapter on "Church Planting and the Structures of the Church" fascinating. Murray starts by stating, "Church planting offers fresh opportunities to think radically about church buildings" (p. 203).

Neighbour, Jr., Ralph W. *Where Do We Go from Here? A Guidebook for the Cell Group Church.* Houston, Tex.: Touch Outreach Ministries, 1990. Nomadic Churches of the "cell group" and even of the "program base design" will benefit from this volume. It has already become somewhat of a classic for its comprehensive yet practical overview of a cell (small group) ministry paradigm, which many Nomadic Churches have (and need) because of their ministry circumstances. The quarterly *Cell Group Journal* available at www.touchusa.org is also sometimes helpful.

Pahl, Jon. *Shopping Malls and Other Sacred Spaces: Putting God in Place.* Grand Rapids: Brazos, 2003. This book will open the patient reader's eyes to a new way of thinking about the interplay of physical place and spiritual discovery, particularly of God's character but extendable to God's people and their place(s) of congregation. Not for bedtime reading!

Parrott, Leslie. *Serving as a Church Greeter*. Grand Rapids: Zondervan, 2002. Albeit brief, this work is loaded with practical tips that can offset some facility-induced limitations and liabilities. It's also useful for training greeters, a position of perhaps even greater import to the Nomadic Church than to its stationary sisters.

Portable Church Industries. *Optimizing the Portable Church*. 14 min. 2001. Videocassette. Through their consultations and customized packages, PCI uses its training and experience to help Nomadic Churches make the most of their housing situation. Despite its brevity and marketing nature, this video sheds some light on some site-specific issues Nomadic Churches should consider. Log on to www.portablechurch.com for more information. *Inc.*, which recognized PCI as 255 on the 2000 *Inc.* 500 Index of fastest growing American companies, also gives a good overview of the company (see Leigh Buchanan, "Assemblies of God," *Inc.*, 1 November 2000, www.inc.com/magazine/20001101/20902. html).

Postma, Gayla R. "Banner Up." *Your Church*, Nov/Dec 2000. www.christianitytoday.com/yc/2000/006/5.28.html. This is a useful primer on creating or purchasing decorative banners that convey meaning and enliven the atmosphere of the meeting site. Links to purchase pre-fabricated banners are also supplied. (*Your Church*, a free publication targeted to church decision makers, periodically provides other items of interest to Nomadic Churches, because in a personal interview the editor acknowledged that about 6 percent of their readers serve in churches who don't have a building.)

Schaller, Lyle E. *44 Ways to Increase Church Attendance*. Nashville: Abingdon Press, 1988. Despite its age, this book offers many easily implementable ideas that can counter some of the adverse effects of mobility. Several of the eleven issues raised in the discussion of the physical site are areas in which Nomadic Churches can make strategic adjustments to attain the desired effect.

Schuchmann, Jennifer. "Church in a Box: Everything a Portable Church Needs on a Sunday Morning for Quick Setup and Storage." *Your Church*, Jan/Feb 2000, 10-12, 14. Crisp, practical, and centered squarely on the Nomadic Church, this arti-

174

cle is a rare—albeit brief—gem. Based on interviews with seasoned nomadic leaders, it surfaces several stresses and needs (mostly of the physical type) and offers some suggestions for addressing them.

Sekulow, Jay. *Knowing Your Rights: Taking Back Our Religious Liberties.* Virginia Beach: Liberty, Life, and Family, 1996. On legal rental rights, note especially pp. 5-8—available free with other relevant material at the American Center of Law and Justice's site (www.aclj.org). This covers the favorable implications of the landmark *Lamb's Chapel* case, which the Supreme Court upheld in *Good News Club v. Milford Central School* (2001). Other pertinent legal issues can be learned from the Rutherford Institute (www.rutherford.org) and the Freedom Forum (www.freedomforum.org; also see "Links to Legal Issues" at www.newchurches.com/legal.htm).

Slaybaugh, RaeAnn. "The Future Is Wide Open: Crossroads Community Is a Church on the Move—in More Ways Than One." *Church Business,* Oct 2000. www.church business.com/articles/0a1profi. html. Here's a quick read with a successful Nomadic Church's marketing advice. *Church Business* is worth scanning for other timely topics (e.g., "Need Space Now? You Don't Have to Sacrifice Form or Function in a Pinch," www.churchbusiness.com/articles/9b1Feat1.html).

Theodore, Jr., Peter C. "A Discovery of the Facility-Related Challenges and Responses of Growing 'Portable Churches' in the Greater Washington, D.C. Area" (D.Min. diss., Biblical Theological Seminary, 2001). This dissertation, which sparked further research for this book, is the only doctoral study to date that focuses exclusively on issues of prime interest to Nomadic Churches. The ambitious person desiring further information than space affords in this book can obtain a copy at www.tren.com (CDs are $20).

Toler, Stan, and Alan Nelson. *The Five Star Church: Serving God and His People with Excellence.* Ventura, Calif.: Regal, 1999. Without mentioning them, the authors present much that Nomadic Churches can apply. Their resounding call to excellence includes an appeal to "Develop Quality Teams," to "Sweat the Small Stuff: Attention to Detail, Efficiency, and Effectiveness," and to maintain "Quality in the Physical

Arena." A rewarding idea is to solicit a "secret shopper" to evaluate the church on a Sunday morning.

Towns, Elmer, C. Peter Wagner, and Thom S. Rainer. *The Everychurch Guide to Growth: How Any Plateaued Church Can Grow.* Nashville: Broadman and Holman Publishers, 1998. Like Carl George's *How to Break Growth Barriers* (e.g., pp. 50-53, 137-43), this work addresses the critical role facilities can play in growing past an attendance plateau. However, it goes beyond the simplistic suggestion to "building a bigger and nicer building" to tactics attainable by many Nomadic Churches of various sizes.

U.S. Government. Small Business Administration. www.sba.gov. Although most churches don't customarily look to government for help, time surfing this site can be well spent. It addresses starting businesses, management, strategic planning, financing, marketing, demographics, communication, technology, resource management, inventorying, goal setting, and other practical topics, facts sheets, workbooks, and sample policies and forms. Most items are free. For example, church planters can use sections of the "Small Business Startup Kit" (www.sba.gov/starting_business/startup/guide.html).

van der Harst, Pete, and Dana L. Cadman. "Real Ministry Need Not Wait for a Building." *Technologies for Worship* (Nov 1995). www.tfwm.com/twm/articles/general/4.html. Van der Harst, founder of Portable Church Industries (see above), and a technical writer surface a few challenges and advantages of the portable church paradigm in this brief piece.

Warren, Rick. *The Purpose-Driven Church: Growth Without Compromising Your Message and Mission.* Grand Rapids: Zondervan, 1995. Nomadic Churches are missional churches! Even if one does not subscribe to all that Saddleback Community Church does, this book is still one of the best introductions to developing a contemporary ministry driven by timeless priorities rather than facilities or lesser motives. Warren offers other helpful insights at www.pastors.com.

White, James Emery. *Opening the Front Door: Worship and Church Growth.* Nashville: Convention Press, 1992. Much of the data in this well-researched volume can fortify Nomadic Churches where they need it most. Far from just a theoretical

176

work on the role of worship in a church's expansion, it offers useful suggestions for enhancing physical surroundings, quality, atmosphere, treatment of guests, variety, and scheduling. Some of its best material addresses the timely realms of visitor attraction, retention, and overall ministry excellence. Best of all, churches can actually *implement* many ideas without owning a building.

Whitson, B. Alan. *327 Questions to Ask Before You Sign a Lease.* Newport Beach, Calif.: B. Alan Whitson Co., 1996. Never had a seminar or seminary class on signing leases? Let this national real estate consultant be your tutor! You'll learn the lingo and the right questions to ask, which can spare major inconveniences and losses at the "rental roulette table."

Wingfield, Mark. "New Alternative Springing up for Temporary Worship Space." *National Association of Church Business Administration* (5 May 2001). www.nacba.net/Article/Sprung.htm. Nomadic Churches who own land but are unable (or unwilling) to sink all their dough into a permanent structure may welcome this relatively inexpensive housing alternative. Happily used by a growing number of fellowships (like Saddleback Community Church), the "tabernacle feel" can almost be nostalgic—or at least functional! Illustrations are provided.

APPENDIX B

SAMPLE COMMUNITY CHURCH FACILITY COORDINATOR MINISTRY DESCRIPTION

I. Reason for the Position

The Facility Coordinator (FC) is to manage Sample Community Church's (SCC) facility affairs so as to maximize our spiritual impact, worshipful atmosphere, and Christian witness while minimizing resource expenditures.

II. Requirements for the Position

1. Be one who loves God and supports SCC as evidenced by:
   a. Being a growing disciple of Jesus with godly character.
   b. Being (or being willing to become) a member of SCC.
2. Be a capable team leader and a cooperative team player.
3. Be a self-starter with good time management skills.
4. Be a servant-leader with strong organization, delegation, relational, and administrative skills.
5. Be a positive person with an encouraging spirit.
6. Be able to allot sufficient time and energy to discharge the duties of this position for a minimum of one year.

III. Relationships in the Position

1. Serve under the oversight of the Executive Pastor.
2. Serve in harmony with SCC staff and lay ministers.
3. Serve regularly and equitably with leaders of the facility sub-crews.
4. Serve in a managerial role with current and prospective facility servants.

IV. Responsibilities of the Position
  A. General Responsibilities
    1. Initiate, recruit, organize, oversee, and publicly and privately encourage Assistant FCs and Crew Captains for various facility crews.
    2. Become familiar with all established facility policies and previous FC reports, and develop and execute new policies and procedures to fulfill the duties of this position in an excellent, economical manner.
    3. Submit a written quarterly report to the Executive Pastor.
    4. Strive to maintain healthy, positive relationships with the host(s).
    5. Work with the treasurer to pay contractual obligations on time.
    6. Help secure facilities to house SCC in the event of displacement.
    7. Give input to the Future Facilities Chairman as requested.
  B. Responsibilities Related to SCC's Corporate Facilities
    1. Oversee the weekly storage, transportation, setup, breakdown, and cleanup processes and all related (non-media) matters for "all church" services and special events.
    2. Be the primary point of contact between SCC and our hosts.
    3. Prepare and submit an annual contract to the host and promptly update it as needed.
    4. Work with ministry leaders to allocate meeting space.
    5. Ensure that host janitorial staff receive a Christmas gift and extra compensation for service that falls on a holiday.
  C. Responsibilities Related to SCC's Office Space
    1. Be the main point of contact between SCC and the landlord for such matters as lease agreement and maintenance.
    2. Oversee acquisition and upkeep of SCC's office equipment.
    3. Maintain an up-to-date master schedule for the office

and provide a monthly copy to all ministry leaders. He will mediate space conflicts.

4. Recruit, train, and oversee cleaning personnel.
5. Oversee the distribution, tracking, and collection of office keys.

V. Reimbursement for the Position

The FC usually invests 10-12 hours and is compensated at $100 per week.

APPENDIX C

POINTERS FOR PORTABLE SOUND SYSTEMS

Effective services, programs, and events rely in part upon effective sound systems. David McLain of Capital Communications in Olympia, Washington, has been working with Nomadic Churches for fifteen years. He explains, "There isn't really a standard sound system for a portable church, because there really isn't a standard church."[1] Plus, media technology changes rapidly. So, here are McLain's time-tested principles for selecting an appropriate sound system.

- The system must be simple to set up (consider time constraints).
- The system must be easy to operate (volunteers will run it).
- The system must be articulate (clear and clean sound).
- The system must be flexible (for changing venues).
- The system must be expandable (to meet the church's growth).
- The system must be affordable (not cheap!).
- The system must be reliable (rugged enough for repeated transport).
- The system must be supported (by a resource person you trust).

APPENDIX D

WEB SITE ESSENTIALS FOR NOMADIC CHURCHES

For reasons explained in chapter 9 and hinted at elsewhere, the Internet can be a strong ally of the Nomadic Church. Much could be said about what constitutes an excellent church presence on the information highway, but here are several elements that belong on every effective Nomadic Church's Web site:

1. State the current meeting site, provide a detailed map, and give driving instructions from all directions. Immediately update this information when it changes so that your location remains clear and accurate. Always apologize for the inconvenience of last minute facility switches, but never apologize for the meeting site itself!
2. Give the permanent mailing address and, if applicable, the office suite and future building site address. This subtly communicates a sense of permanence and accessibility.
3. Without cluttering each page, post plenty of pictures of real people. This takes the focus off "place" and puts it on people—where it belongs. (Hint: Don't make your pages so graphic intensive that they take a long time for standard modems to download. Some people won't bother to view the page.)
4. In your text and images, represent as wide a diversity of people as possible without misrepresenting who you really are. This helps answer the question, "Could I fit in here?"
5. Include a narrative on the history of the church, testimonies of changed lives, and the anticipated future direction (vision).

182

Make it interesting, inviting, and realistic. Visitors who are skeptical of a church in temporary facilities sometimes derive assurance about its permanence and vitality from learning the "story" behind the church, its influence in people's lives, and its plans to march forward.

6. Describe all of your ministries and keep them updated. If a surfer questions whether a homeless church can offer anything of personal benefit beyond the worship service, this will provide the answer. A current calendar of events with a specific description, time, place, cost, and contact person opens the front door wider.

7. Give a brief biography and the contact information for each staff member. Key lay leaders can be represented too. This is a way for people to connect with your leaders and understand their commitment.

8. Offer a "virtual tour." The main purpose is to anticipate and answer questions a person might have about what to expect when visiting. Describe what people will see, hear, smell, taste, and do from the time they enter the parking lot to the time they exit it. Accompany this with pictures and, whenever possible, audio or video.[1] This can melt the "fear factor" of a potential inquirer.

APPENDIX E

TIPS FROM TOMATO TRADERS

Shrewd researchers of a topic often explore unique but roughly parallel enterprises to see how their literature and experience might inform their own topic. Although no educational, business, military, or governmental scenario exactly reflects that of the Nomadic Church, there's at least one secular sector that can lend surprising insight into potential difficulties and constructive responsive strategies. We're referring to good old fashioned farmer's markets (FM)!

In these increasingly popular seasonal markets, vendors rent a nontraditional grocery space for a period of time. They load their merchandise in vehicles to "set up shop" on a given day, engage in commerce, pack up, cultivate their crops throughout the week, and return again the following week to repeat the process. In many ways, this process mirrors a Nomadic Church!

Like the majority of Nomadic Church rental hosts, "most markets do not provide any tools for selling products [read 'conducting ministry']. Vendors are expected to provide their own tables, racks, shelter covers. . . ."[1] Other challenges, such as limited operating space, transportation issues, attracting and retaining loyal customers to a nonconventional site, little financial excess, storage restrictions, the need for creativity and flexibility, the inability to significantly manipulate the environment to be more conducive to commerce, and so forth all find parallels with Nomadic Church challenges. Furthermore, most farmer vendors (as well as church leaders) are motivated by much more than mere economic benefit,[2] and both entities are quickly expanding around the nation.[3]

To the degree an individual vendor or vendor unit parallels a Nomadic Church, and the market management its leasing agent (like a church renting space from a school), there is value in FM studies. For example, researchers in Kansas "focused on . . . markets . . . to understand how they were organized and to determine some of the key factors involved in creating and maintaining a healthy market" (Marr and Gast 1989, p. 1). They concluded: "vendors participating in markets with written guidelines, a market coordinator, and some form of organization were more highly satisfied, suggested fewer improvements, and had a more positive outlook for the future of their markets" (p. 11).

Among other things, these conclusions are informative of a healthy relationship between a vendor (or a church) and its facility host. The success of this relationship is instrumental to the smooth operation and "profitability" of both FMs and Nomadic Churches. Studies also recognize the value of written guidelines to govern the market experience (e.g., Hughes and Mattson, p. 9; Marr and Gast, pp. 3-4). They say that when fair guidelines are known by all parties in advance, consented to before space is leased, and enforced equitably, a more productive relationship develops between the market management and its vendors. The guidelines should address the responsibilities of both parties, fees, operation hours, space parameters, clean up procedures, any restrictions on signs and displays, the termination process, and other pertinent matters. It's equally important for nomadic leaders to request comprehensive written guidelines from their facility host before committing to a lease. Although the guidelines will differ some in focus, they should address similar matters.

Researchers also deem that the most successful FMs have a "market coordinator" for "the enforcement of guidelines, trouble shooting, and serving as a point of contact for vendors" (Hughes and Mattson, p. 11). Likewise, a Nomadic Church may find that having a single host point-of-contact (e.g., a school administrator or head custodian) helps maintain a healthy relationship with the organization, resulting in a longer rental tenure and possible gracious concessions by the host. In all this, "markets [read 'Nomadic Churches'] are successful when there is cooperation, involvement, and communication between all parties" (Marr and Gast 1989, p. 2).

Marr and Gast's "Selling in a Farmer's Market" (pp. 5-7) offers some guidance that, contextualized, can benefit churches (http://ag.arizona.edu/arec/pubs/dmkt/AGuideto.FarmersM.pdf). Principles include paying attention to the atmosphere, not losing the "people touch," involving the family, keeping displays neat, maintaining a positive image, realizing competitors (other churches!) are not enemies, building loyalty, and being patient. The pricing and merchandising strategies, suggestions for quality signs, and tips for effective displays are also reasonably applicable. Without other sophisticated research on mobile ministries, this advice serves as sort of a practical primer.

Beyond these points, a consideration of two more key areas will suffice: advertisement and location. Regarding the former, Hughes and Mattson (pp. 7, 19) found that the most successful markets were those that aggressively advertised in a variety of ways (e.g., signs, radio, newspapers, fliers, T-shirts, bags). Similarly, Marr and Gast suggest that a network of groups be developed, informed of the market (or the church), and enlisted to promote it heavily.[4] The publicity, among other things, attracts people who would not otherwise know where the market is located, when it operates, or what it offers. Without a permanent building to silently announce its existence around the clock, the Nomadic Church must also tenaciously advertise, through a variety of forums, where it meets, when it meets, what it offers, and the like.

Regarding location, Zimet writes, "In the event that the market site is not on a major thoroughfare, its location should be well known and easy to reach."[5] Data collected by Hughes and Mattson indicate "that attendance drops when consumers have to travel over five miles to reach the market" (p. 6). Moreover, "a location that is visible, accessible, with adequate parking nearby and room for expansion should be considered. Market customers appreciate easy access to, and adequate space for, nearby parking. This should include a safe entry with good visibility of the parking area" (Marr and Gast, pp. 2-3).

When choosing a rental site, a church should also consider its visibility, potential expandability (e.g., the addition of more class space), adequate parking, and convenience and accessibility to its intended target audience.[6] Although many people are willing to drive more than five miles to attend church, the principle is presumably valid: The closer a church is to its intended "customer base" and the more the church considers their comfort and needs, the larger and more loyal their "patronage" will likely be.

One must frankly acknowledge that a Nomadic Church is not a FM and vice versa. The former has congregants; the latter has customers. The "bottom line" of the former is measured by conversion and sanctification, the latter by money and self-fulfillment. The former is an expression of the indestructible Body of Christ that Jesus is building (Matt 16:18), while the latter is a temporary exchange of products for profit. Nevertheless, the analogous properties between the two indicate that data from these portable commerce centers can benefit Nomadic Churches, provided they are appropriately filtered and adapted to local church ministry. So, the next time you're out for a weekend drive near a farmer's market, stop and look for more than ripe tomatoes. Look for ministry tips!

THREE PRIMARY SOURCES FOR NOMADIC CHURCHES

Although appendix A lists numerous resources that benefit churches in rented meeting facilities, three deserve special mention.

Portable Church Industries. In the last decade, this innovative company—named to the 2000 "*Inc.* 500 Index" of fastest-growing American companies—has helped over 325 Nomadic Churches in just about every U.S. state optimize their ministry. Their consultations tell you what you need, their customized packages deliver goods to meet those needs, and their training equips you with skills to meet those needs. Recently, a typical package for a 200- to 300-seat church ranged from $50,000 to $70,000, although founder and president Pete van der Harst stresses that no two church packages are alike and expenses can vary widely because they strive to tailor their services for each client. "Efficiency upgrades" that blend your existing equipment with their innovative system are also available. Log on to www.portablechurch.com for more information.

Passion for Planting (Mobile Church Solutions). New Life Christian Church, a flourishing multicampus church in Virginia, started this nonprofit ministry to help Nomadic Churches like themselves. It is part of an overall strategy for church plants that provides church planters with economical, quality products and services for their needs regarding portable equipment (www.church-equipment.com), project management (www.church-planting.net), and marketing (www.church-marketing.com). The overarching organization is Passion for Planting (www.church-planting.net). For several excellent free tools, see www.church-marketing.com/churchplanting.htm.

Easum, Bandy, and Associates. "Renting Space." www.easum-bandy.com/FAQS/renting_space.htm. As part of the more than 2,000 pages of free resources on the site of this premier consulting and equipping organization, this link will take you to some other Nomadic Churches and, more important, their field-tested advice about doing church in rented facilities. E-mail us at Easum@easumbandy.com to add your own thoughts.

NOTES

1. Why the Nomadic Church?

1. Helen T. Gray, "Portable Church: Portable Churches Are the Way to Go for Small and Growing Congregations," *Kansas City Star*, 9 February 2001, sec. E, 1.

2. During an interview with Pastor Kevin Marsico of North Star Community Church (www.northstarcommunitychurch.com) in Ijamsville, Maryland, he told us that at a major church planting conference he attended in the spring of 2001, over one hundred new and seasoned church planters stood up to accept a challenge never to pastor a church in its own facility. Although some could be classified as "traditional," many churches who desire to stay in rented facilities for the duration of their existence are committed to some variety of the cell church (e.g., Ralph W. Neighbour, Jr., *Where Do We Go from Here? A Guidebook for the Cell Group Church* [Houston, Tex.: Touch Outreach Ministries, 1990]), meta-church (e.g., Carl F. George, *The Coming Church Revolution* [Grand Rapids: Revell, 1994]), home church (e.g., Robert and Julia Banks, *The Church Comes Home* [Peabody, Mass.: Hendrickson, 1998]), or "multi-campus" church (Bill Easum and Dave Travis, *Beyond the Box* [Loveland, Colo.: Group, 2003]).

3. Coal Creek Chapel; Bellevue, Wash. (www.coalcreekchapel.org).

4. Mark Chaves, *National Congregations Study* (University of Arizona, 18 May 1998); http://saints-denis.library.arizona.edu/natcong/freq.html. For a discussion of advantages and disadvantages of the most common meeting sights, see Aubrey Malphurs, *Planting Growing Churches for the 21st Century: A Comprehensive Guide for New Churches and Those Desiring Renewal* (Grand Rapids: Baker, 1998), 322-33.

5. The largest survey of congregations every conducted in America found that 10.1 percent of churches have other congregations using their building space for worship (Carl S. Dudley and David A. Roozen, *Faith Communities Today: A Report on Religion in the United States* [March

190

2001]; www.fact.hartsem.edu/topfindings/topicalfindings.htm; see "II. History, Location, and Building").

6. More specifically, all the congregations launched between 1966 and 1989 total only 7 percent more of the total congregations in America today than churches started between 1990 and 2000 (Dudley and Roozen, *Faith Communities Today*. See link to Web site above). According to a study by Columbia University, the late 1900s saw the launching of one new church every three weeks—just in the South Bronx of New York City! (Tony Carnes, "New York's New Hope," *Christianity Today*, Dec 2004, p. 34.)

7. For example, Lyle Schaller described churches that "use temporary facilities" as "new congregations serving people from the lower half of the income structure" (*Growing Plans: Strategies to Increase Your Church's Membership* [Nashville: Abingdon Press, 1983], 150). He also delineated thirteen reasons why a church should *not* plan to remain in rented facilities. Schaller should be commended for at least raising the issue of churches meeting in rented facilities, something few of his colleagues had done at that time.

8. From an e-mail Rick Warren sent to authors on 11/09/2003.

9. For one of many examples—this one from a secular news source—see Leila Fadel, "Disenchanted with Sanctuaries and Traditional Services, Some Young Worshippers Feel More Comfortable in Coffee Shops, Bars, Homes," (May 1, 2004); www.theledger.com/apps/pbcs.dll/article?AID=/20040501/NEWS/405010318/1021.

10. Tim Downley, *Introduction to the History of Christianity* (Minneapolis: Fortress Press, 2002), 77-79.

11. See April M. Washington and Linda Stewart Ball, "Houses of the Holy: Church Construction in Collin County Reaches an All-Time High," *Plano Morning News*, 27 January 2001, 1-2. This figure includes synagogues and mosques.

12. The Baptist General Convention of Texas addresses this issue this way: "The average church pays for space 168-hours a week, yet uses it only eight. New churches can't afford that luxury. A portable church costs much less than a fixed site. For example, a church with monthly rent of only $1,416.00 provides a capacity for over 2,000 people a week. That's the equivalent mortgage payment for a 400-seat facility. A portable church gives the new church time to start a building program at the right time. Most of the nationally known mega-churches started with . . . years as a portable church" (*Using a Portable Church* [1996–1999]; www.bgct.org/csc/Portable.html).

13. See these and related statistics compiled on the church planting resource page of the Open Bible Churches (http://www.openbiblecentral.org/planting/planting.htm).

14. Ray Bowman, *When Not to Build: An Architect's Unconventional Wisdom for the Growing Church* (rev. and exp.; Grand Rapids: Baker, 2000).

15. Stuart Murray, *Church Planting: Laying Foundations* (Great Britain: Paternoster Press, 1998), 208; also see pp. 206-10.

Notes

2. Biblical Truth for the Nomadic Church

1. Since the temple was built at God's command, these important Old Testament verses, which Stephen and Paul later expanded upon, are "not a condemnation of earthly temples as such, but a condemnation of the idea that God can be confined to and is satisfied with such an abode" (Edward J. Young, *The Book of Isaiah*, 3 vols. [Grand Rapids: Eerdmans, 1972], 3:518). Even in this era, the temple was not intended to be permanent nor the lone place of God's presence!

2. The Samaritan woman's question about the proper place of worship is only of marginal interest to Jesus, because both the geographical place (Jerusalem) and structural place of worship (the temple) were presently fading into obscurity (see John 4:7-26). God's spiritual essence, omnipresence, and unfolding plan negate the presumption that *any* building or place is more appropriate for worship than any other: "This is worship not tied to holy places but impacted by a holy Person. . . . Jesus is announcing a new immediacy with God that will not be mediated through place, but rather through the Spirit" (Gary M. Burge, *John*, NIV Application Commentary [Grand Rapids: Zondervan, 2000], 147, 158). Hendrickson summarizes: "Jesus answers that not where one worships matters but the attitude of heart and mind and the obedience to God's truth regarding the object and method of worship is what matters" (*The Gospel of John*, New Testament Commentary [Grand Rapids: Baker, 1953], 166).

3. *The Gospel According to John*, New International Commentary on the New Testament (Grand Rapids: Eerdmans, 1971), 267.

4. Edmund Clowney, *The Church*, Contours of Christian Theology (Downers Grove, Ill.: IVP, 1995), 123-24.

5. If anything, the focus is on a specified day ("the Lord's Day"—Acts 20:7; Rev 1:10), rather than on a designated place ("if the whole church comes together . . . if an unbeliever or someone who does not understand comes in"—1 Cor 14:23-24). This is evident even when the place is not "ideal," as in Acts 20:8-12 where the oxygen depravation and warmth due to the "many lamps in the upper room where they were gathered" (v. 8) likely led to Eutychus's sleepy fall. Likewise, Luke—who is fond of providing precise details—merely notes that at Pentecost the fledgling group of believers "were all together in one place" (Acts 2:1): "His emphasis is on the 'when' and not at all on the 'where' of the event" (Richard N. Longnecker, "Acts," in *Expositor's Bible Commentary*, vol. 9, ed. Frank E. Gaebelein [Grand Rapids: Zondervan, 1981], 269). This perspective on the assembly of believers persists throughout the New Testament (e.g., Heb 10:25—"Let us not give up meeting together . . ."—wherever that may be).

6. Stemming from its earliest usage, the basic sense of this term is "assembly" (Walter Bauer, *A Greek-English Lexicon of the New Testament and Other Early Christian Literature*, rev. and aug. by William F. Arndt and F. Wilbur Gingrich, 2nd ed. rev. and aug. from

Bauer's 5th ed. by F. Wilbur Gingrich and Frederick W. Danker [Chicago: University of Chicago Press, 1979], 240-41). In the New Testament, it came to represent "the full-blown technical designation for the Christian people of God," that is, those who profess faith in and allegiance to Christ, regardless of if they are actually gathered in assembly (Robert L. Saucy, *The Church in God's Program* [Chicago: Moody, 1972], 15). Notably, of its 114 occurrences in Scripture the word never refers to a church building, nor do Jesus' only two uses of it presuppose, suggest, or require any particular meeting place (Matt 16:18; 18:17). The same is true of the other New Testament writers.

7. These places include public sites, personal residences, and the open air (e.g., Acts 2:46; 12:12; 16:13; 17:17, 19; 18:28; 20:20; Rom 16:5; 1 Cor 16:19; Phlm 2). This is entirely in line with the practice of Jesus, who primarily gathered and ministered among his disciples in homes and other "non-religious" places (cf. Matt 8:14-15; 9:10, 23; 17:25; 26:6; 17ff; Mark 2:1-12, 15ff; 3:20; 5:38; 7:17, 24; 9:28, 33; 10:10; 14:12-21; Luke 5:18, 29; 7:10, 36-37; 10:38; 14:1; 22:12ff; John 13-16; 20:26; Acts 1:12-13). Indeed, rather than build special facilities, "for almost three hundred years [until Constantine's erection of the first Christian basilicas after the 313 Edict of Milan] the believers met in homes, not in synagogues or edifices constructed for the sole purpose of religious assembly" (Bradley B. Blue, "Architecture, Early Church," in *Dictionary of the Later New Testament and Its Developments*, eds. Ralph P. Martin and Peter H. Davids [Downers Grove, Ill.: IVP, 1997], 91, 95). Yet even then—through today—homes and a wide assortment of other nonreligious buildings were fully adequate to facilitate their occupants' biblical mandates (e.g., see Robert and Julia Banks, *The Church Comes Home* [Peabody, Mass.: Hendrickson, 1998], 49-73).

8. R. Kevin Seasoltz, *The House of God: Sacred Art and Church Architecture* (New York: Herder and Herder, 1963), 63. It is true that Abraham's nomadic lifestyle led him—like Noah before him and Isaac and Jacob after him—to establish altars "to worship the Lord and commemorate the Lord's presence at that place" (Tremper Longman, *Immanuel in Our Place: Seeing Christ in Israel's Worship* [Phillipsburg, N.J.: P&R, 2001], 20). Yet the fact that these pre-Mosaic altars were initially "rough improvised structures" consisting of "the materials most easily obtained in the field" did not diminish their spiritual value (Harold M. Wiener, "Altar," in *The International Standard Bible Encyclopedia*, rev. ed., ed. G. W. Bromiley [Grand Rapids: Eerdmans, 1991], 127). Likewise, the comparatively "rough improvised structures" that many modern Nomadic Churches use as meeting places do not diminish the structures' value as a place of corporate worship.

9. The ark where God met Moses was not God's dwelling place *per se*, but was the sign of the Lord's presence in the midst of the covenant community (cf. Exod 29:45-46; Num 7:8-9; 2 Sam 6:2; 2 Kgs 19:15; 1 Chr 13:6; Ps 80:1; 99:1; 132:7-8; Isa 37:16; Ezek 9:3; Heb 9:5). God was present everywhere—in Egypt, on Mt. Sinai, in Canaan, and beyond

Notes

(see Yves M. J. Congar, "The Presence of God at the Time of the Exodus and in the Lifetime of Moses," *The Mystery of the Temple* [Westminster, Md.: Newman Press, 1962], 3-19). The tabernacle's establishment represents an escalation from the "occasional appearance of God" to an "ongoing presence" with the people (Terence E. Fretheim, *Exodus*, Interpretation [Louisville: John Knox, 1991], 264). This becomes a "permanent presence" with the advent of "'Immanuel'—which means 'God with us'" (Matt 1:23; cf. Isa 7:14; Matt 28:20; John 1:14; 14:23).

10. Peter Enns, *Exodus*, NIV Application Commentary (Grand Rapids: Zondervan, 2000), 555.

11. Evidence of this is seen in nearly every aspect of the tabernacle, from the intricate priestly vestments to the sixty-nine ornaments on the lampstand alone (cf. Walter C. Kaiser, Jr., "Exodus," in *Expositor's Bible Commentary*, vol. 2, ed. Frank E. Gaebelein [Grand Rapids: Zondervan, 1990], 457-58). Perhaps the greatest evidence of the importance of this is that the first clear mention of the Spirit's filling is in connection with the artistic design and craftsmanship of the tabernacle (Exod 28:3; 31:1-11; 35:30-35).

12. This is not to say that the tabernacle was particularly light. In fact, following R. B. Y. Scott on Hebrew weights and their modern equivalents, Brevard Childs estimates that the precious metals alone weighed close to 13,000 pounds (*The Book of Exodus: A Critical, Theological Commentary*, Old Testament Library [Philadelphia: Westminster, 1974], 637). The point is that God did not make it any heavier than necessary by adding a heavy structure (roof, walls, and floor) but viewed curtains as sufficient.

13. Even the number of carts and oxen for transportation were appointed. The Gershonites were granted two wagons drawn by four oxen (Num 7:7), while the Merarites used four wagons drawn by eight oxen (v. 8). It makes sense—and for a Nomadic Church, too—that greater transportation capabilities be allocated to the crew(s) with responsibility for the larger and heavier items.

14. Ronald Allen notes that "all the preparation suggests a rigorous training schedule before actual work would be done." This "may account for the distinction of twenty-five years of age in 8:24 and thirty years in 4:3. That intervening five-year period may have been a time of intense internship" ("Numbers," in *Expositor's Bible Commentary*, vol. 2, ed. Frank E. Gaebelein [Grand Rapids: Zondervan, 1990], 734). For optimal performance, Nomadic Churches should not slight leader development or worker training either!

3. Challenges Facing the Nomadic Church

1. Struggles the early church faced range from external persecution unto death to internal disagreement, doctrinal impurity, and organizational dilemmas. Evidence of these ordeals and the ensuing growth through them is reflected in virtually every chapter of Acts (cf. 2:13; 4:1-

Notes

3, 17-18; 5:1-10, 17-18; 6:1-4, 9-14; 7:54-58; 8:1-3; 9:1-2, 23; 12:1-6; 13:6-8, 45, 50; 14:1-6, 19; 15:1-41; 16:16-24; 17:1-9, 18, 32; 18:5-6; 19:23-41; 20:29-31; 21:23-36; 22:4-5, 23-25; 23:12-15; 25:2-3ff; 26:9-11, 24; and 27:11-44). Nomadic leaders can learn a lot from studying how these earliest Christian pioneers handled their obstacles.

4. Revealing Physical and Personnel Challenges

1. From an e-mail sent by executive pastor Mark Stephens to Pete Theodore on 4 December 2001.
2. In addition to working to have a good relationship, leaders also strongly agreed that they express gratitude to those from whom they rent and its personnel, despite acknowledging negative experiences with the host and its agents. Based on this and our follow-up probing, we conclude that—at least from the churches' perspectives—the host is primarily responsible for most lapses in the host-tenant relationship.
3. RaeAnn Slaybaugh, "The Future Is Wide Open: Crossroads Community Is a Church on the Move—in More Ways Than One," *Church Business* (Oct 2000); www.churchbusiness.com/articles/0a1profi.html.
4. In comparatively few instances, churches can remain in the same facility for many years. Conversely, some seem to move every year. On average, however, we've found that the median stay for a Nomadic Church in the same facility is under two years. For various reasons, including numerical growth and experience gained through "trial and error," moves are typically more frequent in a church's earlier years than in its latter years.

5. Responding to Physical and Personnel Challenges

1. "Real Ministry Need Not Wait for a Building," *Technology for Worship Magazine* (Nov. 1995); www.tfwm.com/twm/articles/general/4.html.
2. For a complete look at team-based ministry, see "Team Based Ministries Workbook" at www.easumbandy.com. While there, review "team based ministries" in the FAQs section of the Free Resources. Appendix A offers other recommended resources on the subject.
3. In all the hustle and bustle of setting up and breaking down, a church has to be proactive in order not to miss redemptive opportunities. New Hope Christian Fellowship has one of the best decision registering booths we've seen. To view it, go to www.easumbandy.com/resources/index.php?action=searchresults&pl_option[1]=5&keywords=&searchsectiona=e-h. Another excellent example is found at www.connectionpower.com.
4. RaeAnn Slaybaugh, "Stump the Facility Manager? I Think Not," *Church Business*, January 2001, 27-28. Notice how this organization esteems its members as engaged in "ministry" not mere "maintenance." Members of the NACFM serve churches with buildings, but the materi-

als they offer can still sometimes benefit facility coordinators in portable churches (see www.nacfm.org).

5. In addition to arranging chairs to block out distractions, research has shown that the shape of the meeting space and arrangement of the furniture directly affect the communication process. Mark L. Knapp's studies led him to introduce the concept of a "zone of participation," which is roughly in the shape of a wide diamond with the speaker at one point on the long end (*Nonverbal Communication* [New York: Holt, Rinehart, and Winston, 1972], 26-29). People seated within this diamond zone are most likely to respond to what is being said and done in the pulpit area. This means that square and long rectangular areas are less conducive to effective communication between a speaker and those seated outside of this zone. Nomadic Churches can factor this into their facility selection. Or, if seating is adjustable at the site, a curved or semicircular arrangement will better facilitate communication.

6. Nomadic leaders report many benefits to a strong relationship with the host, including a higher probability that doors will be opened on time, the facility will be cleaner, the climate will be more pleasant, custodians will be more attentive to their concerns, more advance notice will be given for facility alterations, the church will be better represented to faculty and administration, there will be less accusations made against the church, supplies and equipment will be made available (sometimes cheaper or without cost), some storage space will be granted, the church will not be charged for minimally overstaying its contract period on a given Sunday, cleaning and construction will be scheduled at times that interfere less with church functions, the facility will be granted for special events, and lost items will be returned.

7. Responding to Program and Special Event Challenges

1. Mike Breaux, "Canyon Ridge: 2 Years Later," *The Visionary,* February 1995; www.gycm.org/visionary/plants/canyonridge.htm. Read the stories of other Nomadic Churches at this site for church planting in the Northeast.

2. See Tom Zind, "California Congregation Equips 'Portable Church,'" *Presenting Communications* (23 August 2000); www.info-comm.org/newsnetwork/Installations/index.cfm?objectID=B9CCD04F-CB08-11D4-A09800D0B7913DE7.

3. "Portable baptisteries" are available for the motivated church (see Katherine Crosett, "Furnishings That Fit: Movable Classrooms, Custom Baptisteries, Sound Baffles, and More," *Your Church,* September/October 2000, 22-24, 26). But because they require a large amount of storage, transportation, time, and manpower, Nomadic Churches tend to shy away from them. Besides, meaningful alternative arrangements can be made.

4. For more on Sidewalk Sunday School, see the Web sites www.sidewalksundayschool.com and http://easumbandy.com/resources/

index.php?action=details&record=537. Get introduced to the ministry of Child Evangelism Fellowship at www.cefonline.com. Of course, you can always develop your own off-site seasonal children's program, like Seneca Creek Community Church did with their innovative "Happy Birthday, Jesus!" parties held in members' homes.

8. Revealing Visitor and Financial Challenges

1. Lyle Schaller, *44 Ways to Increase Church Attendance* (Nashville: Abingdon Press, 1988), 92. More recently, pastor Andy Stanley of North Point Community Church (www.northpoint.org) in Alpharetta, Georgia, is credited with saying that one of "three things [that] are critical to your effectiveness in reaching those who have yet to make a personal commitment to Christ" is an "appealing context" (Ken Godevenos, "Meeting Unique Needs: Your Maintenance/Facilities Supervisor," *Church Business,* July 2004; www.churchbusiness.com/articles/471staff.html).

2. In 2000, the average American church spent about 20 percent of their budget on facilities, including rent, utilities, mortgage, and upkeep (Eric Reed, "Where the Money Goes," *Leadership Journal* [Spring 2000]: 88-90). That percentage is mirrored and occasionally exceeded by Nomadic Churches, especially larger ones in high-rent areas who use more than a Sunday rental site.

9. Responding to Visitor and Financial Challenges

1. Jennifer Schuchmann, "Church in a Box: Everything a Portable Church Needs on a Sunday Morning for Quick Setup and Storage," *Your Church*, January/February 2000, 11.

2. Many resources produced over the last decade give insight into this and related subjects, including John P. Jewell's recent work, *Wired for Ministry: How the Internet, Visual Media, and Other New Technologies Can Serve Your Church* (Grand Rapids: Brazos, 2004).

3. Recently, some have called congregations who intentionally do this "externally focused churches." Because of their unique housing context, Nomadic Churches are ideally suited to be outwardly focused servants in their community. For more on the philosophy behind this refreshing phenomenon and pointers for adopting it, see Rick Rusaw and Eric Swanson, *The Externally Focused Church* (Loveland, Colo: Group Publishing, 2004).

4. See Ray Bowman, *When Not to Build* in appendix A for a penetrating discussion of what a building can and *can't* do. Chapter 8 of Stuart Murray's *Church Planting: Laying Foundations* (Carlisle, U.K.: Paternoster, 1998) is similarly insightful.

5. Pastors and staff who work from their homes will become less conspicuous as well. Interestingly, the trend of home-based employment was recently collaborated by a poll conducted at Monster.com. Out of

64,374 votes, 71 percent voted "yes" when asked, "Do you see yourself working full-time from home in the next three years?" (http://forums.monster.com/poll.asp?pollid=145).

6. For a practical discussion of the "treatment of guests," see the chapter by that title in James White's *Opening the Front Door: Worship and Church Growth* (Nashville: Convention Press, 1992).

7. "Real Ministry Need Not Wait for a Building," *Technologies for Worship* (Nov 1995); www.tfwm.com/twm/articles/general/4.html. These savings are more apparent when you factor in buying land, designing a facility, erecting a building, furnishing the site, paying a new mortgage and taxes, and maintaining and expanding the property.

8. In 1990 George Barna reported that "the average church in America allocates about 5 percent of its budget for evangelism, but approximately 30 percent of its budget for buildings and maintenance" (*The Frog in the Kettle* [Ventura, Calif.: Regal, 1990], 142-43). Interestingly, we found that on balance growing Nomadic Churches spend considerably more on evangelism and less on facilities. A homeless church that practices missional budgeting has a pair of powerful assets that can make them a true Great Commission church!

9. See Chris Maag, "Church without a Home: Antioch Bible Church Has More Than 3,000 Members, but It Doesn't Have a Building of Its Own," *EastSide Journal*, 5 December 1999; www.eastsidejournal.com/sited/retrstory.pl/7156.

10. For more on understanding and developing corporate mission statements, see Thomas G. Bandy, *Moving Off the Map* (Nashville: Abingdon Press, 1998).

10. It's All in the Attitude

1. Jay E. Adams, *The Christian Counselor's Manual: The Practice of Nouthetic Counseling* (Grand Rapids: Zondervan, 1973), 115. Barry D. Smith and Harold J. Vetter label what we have perceived from our study participants as "phenotypical dispositions"; that is, "current, important consistencies in behavior" that are neither genotypical (dispositions that are basic and fundamental to the personality) nor pseudo (erroneous, superficial dispositions); (*Theoretical Approaches to Personality* [Englewood Cliffs, N.J.: Prentice Hall, 1982], 145).

2. On a related note, we discovered a strong "attitude of gratitude" among participants. No matter how intense the limitations of a particular meeting site are, leaders strongly agree that they are grateful for being able to meet where they do. Like other attitudes, their thankfulness is expressed in tangible action toward the host (see chapter 5). Nomadic pastor Doepel says it well: "Being mobile makes sure you never take anything for granted" (RaeAnn Slaybaugh, "The Future Is Wide Open: Crossroads Community Is a Church on the Move—in More Ways Than One," *Church Business* [October 2000]).

3. See chapter 2. Other literature on Nomadic Churches also con-

firms this attitude. For example, a successful pastor writes, "One of the most important things we've learned first-hand is that 'church' is not something you come to it's something you are! That lesson has been invaluable and has given a strong foundation and philosophy for ministry" (Mike Breaux, "Canyon Ridge: 2 Years Later," *The Visionary* [February 1995], 3). Lewis's first of eight principles for Nomadic Churches is "Be the Church Now" (Brad Lewis, "The Portable Church." *Vital Ministry* [Mar/Apr 1999], 1-2. www.onlinerev.com/article.asp? ID=109), which includes this quotation from a nomadic pastor: "Our people can get tired really fast. It's not easy to feel like a church without a building, so I try to say something every week that reminds our people that this is a church—you are a church" (p. 5).

4. The lead pastor of one bustling Nomadic Church notes, "You are constantly having to be flexible, creative, positive, and on the move" (Mike Breaux, "Canyon Ridge: 2 Years Later," *The Visionary* [February 1995], 2). Another adds: "We've learned to be flexible. We live by the words, 'Yes, it's probably going to change!'" (Lewis, "Portable Church," 1).

5. Rick Warren, the prime developer of the purpose-driven ministry philosophy that balances the five major purposes of a Christian church (most of which he formulated while pastoring a Nomadic Church), explains that it is as much attitude as it is action. For instance, Warren refers to this model as "a guiding force, a controlling assumption, a directing conviction behind everything that happens . . . a new perspective" (*Purpose-Driven Church* [Grand Rapids: Zondervan, 1995], 77, 80). Such terms are at the center of the definition of "attitude" (see above), and this has served Warren's church well: "Our resistance to building buildings has been one of Saddleback's values since its inception twenty-one years ago. One of the goals we set at Saddleback was to prove that you don't need to build a building in order to grow a church. That's why we waited until after our congregation was averaging over 10,000 in attendance before we built our first building! I think we proved our point" (Rick Warren, "The Church's Edifice Complex" [July 2001]; www.pastors.com/RWMT/?id=25&artid=1225&expand=1).

6. This mindset that facilities are for the purpose of impacting people extends to future permanent facilities as well, as seen in the following excerpts from the building/stewardship campaigns from two churches we studied:

> We have a vision for what Bay Area will be in the future. Not just a vision of a building, but a vision of a faithful people. . . . We envision a place that can be a blessing to you, your family, each other, and a place that can be a blessing to the world. . . . This is not about a building. It's about people; people coming to faith. People maturing in their faith and impacting the world for Christ.

. . . Ultimately it is about continuing to grow as a family with passion for God and compassion for the world. It's about seeing lives transformed for Christ from here to the nations.

The main reason we're engaged in this campaign is because we believe that people matter to God and therefore ought to matter to us. Facilities are simply a means to an end, and the end is people. When it's all said and done, this campaign is all about raising up people and then raising up funds necessary to do a more effective job at reaching seekers, building believers and equipping God's people to impact their world.

7. Other literature on successful Nomadic Churches confirms the priority of prayer. For example, the senior pastor of Coal Creek Church (the seventh daughter church of Overlake Christian Church) posits as the very first principle in their success: "Prayer! You cannot plan better than God can provide! When we work, we work. When we pray, God works. This has been our motto since day one. Pray continually! Someone has been praying and fasting for the ministry of Coal Creek every day since the first Sunday!" (Bryan Carter. "Coal Creek Chapel—Reflections One Year Later," *The Visionary*, February 1995. <http://www.gycm.org/visionary/plants/timeflies.html> [19 August 2001]).

8. However, we *can* say that "Churches That Pray Are Churches That Grow," as a February 2004 report based on research by Thom S. Rainer (and many before him) confirms (see www.churchcentral.com/nw/s/template/Article.html/id/18428).

Appendix A: Resource Recommendations

1. The situation is the same among doctoral research. Compared to the 3,500 accessible Doctor of Ministry and Missiology dissertations at the end of 2003, almost none have churches in temporary facilities as a primary audience, test group, or beneficiary. Among the few that do, the emphasis is upon some aspect of their building acquisition, design, construction, location, or relocation. These writings may well be valuable to churches considering or nearing transition onto a permanent campus. Otherwise, any potential benefit will not be accrued until a time that is *future* from a Nomadic Church's present ministry context. For an exception, see the entry under "Theodore" in the resource list.

Appendix C: Pointers for Portable Sound Systems

1. See McLain's helpful article, "Sacred Sound: Making It Mobile," at www.livesoundint.com/archives/2002/janfeb/portable/portable.php. On the subject, also see www.churchmedia.net/CMU/articles/mediaministry/011.htm and www.essentricaudio.com/portachurch.htm. For more information on sound systems, see www.easumbandy.com in the Free Resource section under FAQs.

Notes

Appendix D: Web Site Essentials for Nomadic Churches

1. For different approaches to virtual tours, see www.senecacreek.org/index.cfm?PAGE_ID=87 (Seneca Creek Community Church), www.abchurch.org/about/about.php (Antioch Bible Church), www.enewhope.org/portal/video/archive.php (New Hope Community Church), www.fcfchurch.com/experience (Fellowship Christian Church), and http://sayingyes.com/ (Pinnacle Church). If you've seen or developed an innovative virtual tour, send the link to us at Easum@easumbandy.com so other Nomadic Churches can benefit.

Appendix E: Tips from Tomato Traders

1. Charles Marr and Karen L. B. Gast, "A Guide to Starting, Operating and Selling in Farmers' Markets," Manhattan: Kansas State University, Cooperative Extension Service, 1989, 2.

2. "Judging from the small amount earned per market day for the work and time involved, it makes sense that vendors would be motivated in several ways, rather than just economically," writes Megan E. Hughes and Richard H. Mattson ("Farmer's Markets in Kansas: A Profile of Vendors and Market Organization," Manhattan: Kansas State University, Agricultural Experiment Station, 1993, 9). In fact, they found that the "farmers valued the social aspects of the market as much as" its other benefits (ibid., 9). A majority viewed "meeting people" to be as strong an attraction to the market as financial gain (ibid., 20).

3. According to the USDA, the number of FMs in America "has grown dramatically, increasing 63 percent from 1994 to 2000. According to the 2000 National Farmers Market Directory, there are over 2,800 farmer's markets operating in the United States" (*Farmer's Market Facts* [updated June 2001]; available online: http://www.ams.usda.gov/farmersmarkets/facts.htm. [9 August 2001]).

4. Within this group could be local editors, area reporters, community development and civic groups, and other local leaders (p. 4). Nomadic Churches, especially new ones, should not overlook this community-based network in their promotion. They should also consider special "promotion events," which in the FM arena may include "special feature days, demonstrations, craftsmen or artisans" (p. 5).

5. David Zimet, "Characteristics of Successful Vegetable Farmers' Retail Markets," *Proceedings of the Florida State Horticulture Society* 99 (Tallahassee: Florida Agricultural Experiment Station, 1986), 30.

6. Interestingly, Barna found that Baby Boomers and "college graduates were less concerned about" things like "how far the church is located from your home," "how comfortable the sanctuary or auditorium is," and "how easy it is to find a parking space at the church" ("Americans Describe Their Ideal Church," *The Barna Update* [7 October 1998]. Available at www.barna.org). Thom Rainer also balances the issue of how important location is through a recent study of

201

thirteen "mediocre congregations that grew to become vibrant, healthy churches without changing pastors. To his surprise, he discovered that there was little correlation between location and growth" ("Your Church's Physical Location Has Little to Do with Growth," *Monday Morning Insight,* September 13, 2004; http://mondaymorninginsight. typepad.com/monday_morning_insight_we/2004/09/your_ churchs_ph.html).